HEALING *RIGHT* NOW

Your On-Ramp to an Effective Healing Ministry

Gary Mayer

Published by Gary L. Mayer
1720 10th Ave. S. Ste. 4-401
Great Falls, MT. 59405
https://facebook.com/GaryMayer.author/

Cover design by Gitit Ezagouri; https://www.behance.net/gitita
Editors: Megan Cordeiro and Jill Higgins

HEALING *RIGHT* NOW/ Gary L. Mayer. -- 1st ed.
ISBN: 9798321123003

Acknowledgements

Over the years I have been taught and discipled by many men, women, and ministries. I want to pay tribute to some of those who have been instrumental in teaching and mentoring me, especially as it relates to divine healing.

In the early days, men like Jack Hayford, JT Dearinger, and Derek Prince were important teachers. From them I learned about the ministry of healing and deliverance and solidified my understanding of Israel and the Church. In my bible college days in London, I drew much from Jean Darnall and Roy Peacock regarding faith and miracles.

While pastoring in the UK, I was privileged to meet Giancarlo Elia and his wife Catherine. It was through their ministry I received a revelation of the Father's love and my identity as His son. He invited me to a Fatherheart Ministry conference in Holland where I met James Jordan, which proved to be a turning point in my relationship with God. I owe much to Giancarlo for being God's instrument in leading me into a revelation of sonship.

More recently, Andrew Wommack and his team of instructors at Charis Bible College, including Barry Bennett and his book *He Healed Them All,* were instrumental in laying a firm foundation in the healing ministry. Barb and I have attended many of the Charis *Healing is Here* conferences either in person or on-line and have learned and experienced much from the wide array of excellent teachers—too many to name.

My wife and I attended in-person training by Curry Blake, leader of the John G. Lake Ministries in Plano, TX. We, as well, completed Henry Wright's course, *For My Life,* to be trained on spiritual roots of disease.

Over the years, books and teachings by Bill Johnson have impacted my life and ministry in many ways. I would be remiss if I didn't give credit to Dutch Sheets for his books and daily blog post, GiveHim15.com. He is discipling the nation in prayer and intercession. Recently Barb and I attended a training conference at Healing Rooms International in Spokane, Washington. We were challenged by the way they lean on the Holy Spirit's leading in healing ministry.

I want to mention Jack Taylor with respect to kingdom of God. We joined Jack and his wife Freda for a week immersed in kingdom teaching, while on a cruise to Alaska. One time I told my wife that if Jack has written a book on anything, I want to read it.

A special mention is in order for my good friend, Dr. Don Crum. Don arrived in our lives just as we were planting our church in England in 1992. He apostolically oversaw our ministry. He taught and modeled the power of God and the authority we have as believers. He ministered in the miraculous and tutored me in the skills of faith and my identity as a king and priest. As we traveled together to Mexico, the Ukraine, and Russia, I observed firsthand the power of God moving through this humble man. I would not be where I am now without the friendship and ministry of Don Crum.

I want to thank Brendan and Sarah Mayer for allowing Barb and I to use the Prayer Room at Siloe Wellness Center in La Mision, Mexico as our first healing room. For nearly three years we took appointments to minister to the local Mexicans. Priscila Cortez was our anointed translator and partner in this adventure. We saw God move powerfully while healing bodies and souls, restoring marriages, saving the lost, and extending the kingdom of God. We learned to work closely with the doctors and nurses and, from time to time, a doctor wrote a prescription to see Pastor Gary and Barb for prayer.

I want to thank the leadership team at New City Church in Great Falls, Montana for welcoming us and trusting me to write a curriculum and teach the contents of this book. Pastor Nate and his team have been very supportive as we have seen God do some marvelous things.

Last, but first of all, is my wonderful wife Barb. She and I have been shoulder-to-shoulder in our growth and understanding of this thing called the Christian life. Truth be told, she is often two steps ahead of me! Her passion for God and thirst for learning have not waned in her forty-six years as a believer. Early in our marriage, our pastor prophetically spoke over us that we have the ministry of Priscilla and Aquila. We work best together, especially in the ministry of healing. Jesus sent His disciples out two by two. It has been that way with us also; two are much better than one. I truly would not be where I am if it were not for Barb's love, dedication, and faithfulness.

Endorsements

It is a tremendous joy to recommend *Healing Right Now* to you. My dear friend and partner in the kingdom, Pastor Gary Mayer, has processed this area of ministry for years and has experienced the outworking of the ministry of healing with all its challenges in a successful way. He communicates in a way that is easily entreated but extremely challenging – which this subject requires. His faithfulness to the Scriptures simply moves the reader and student to a greater faith for healing and miracles.

Gary catches the strength of God's word that surrounds the subject and work of God's miraculous healing. This resource will pull you to Jesus and His love and compassion for people of all kinds and His desire to do "exceedingly, abundantly above all that we could ask or imagine according to His power that's at work in us!"

I especially found myself challenged by chapter eight in that I had, over the years, drifted more to a Church perspective to the neglect of a kingdom perspective. Gary's challenge and clarity of truth about the kingdom now jarred me back to a desire to see the kingdom demonstrated in a much greater measure. I believe you will find chapter eight alone worth the read! It will require some additional work on my part to sort it out and recover the ground I have seceded over the past years.

Healing Right Now is an extremely timely work. The hour demands an operational, functional resource to teach and refresh His church in this desperate arena of ministry. It will communicate and impart the urgency of the hour and a stirring, loving wakeup call for all who call on the name of Jesus! I highly recommend Gary's work to you!

— Pastor Lee Barrows
Associate Pastor, New City Church,
Great Falls Montana

Healing Right Now is one of the best works I've read on the subject of healing in my over fifty-three years of international ministry. It is both scholarly and inspirational. On the scholarly side of the coin, Gary deals head-on with some of the more challenging theological questions regarding the subject of healing today, such as God's sovereignty and "Is it always God's will to heal?" *Healing Right Now*, is biblically sound, but also inspires a practical faith for believing that God is not only *able* to heal but is more than *happy* to heal. I highly recommend *Healing Right Now* as an excellent manual for learning how to partner with God in His healing ministry today.

— Dr. Don Crum
Leadership International

Healing Right Now is a dynamic, insightful, and wonderfully practical guide into the NOW reality of health and healing that Jesus secured for all of us in the atonement. Gary saturated this work with Scripture and grounded its theology in God's word. This book is going to inspire and empower people to walk in and impart the healing grace that Jesus has already accomplished for us all. I am excited to teach through Gary's book at our church and use it for our discipleship programs.

— Pastor Tom Moffett
The Vine Church
Sonoita, AZ.

"Then He called His twelve disciples together and gave them power and authority over all demons, and to cure diseases. He sent them to preach the kingdom of God and to heal the sick."
— LUKE 9:1-2

"For laying aside the commandment of God, you hold the tradition of men ... making the word of God of no effect through your tradition which you have handed down. And many such things you do."
— MARK 7:8, 13

CONTENTS

Preface

For years my wife and I have been studying and equipping ourselves to be more effective in ministering healing to those who are sick and oppressed. I have notes tucked away everywhere ... in my computer, on scraps of paper, and in my spiritual notebooks. Teaching pastors tend to do this. In this learning process we have been blessed to see an increase in healings and freedom.

Recently, we began to teach on this subject in our church in Great Falls, Montana. We were given the opportunity to lead a small group, called *Healing Now*. This forced me to organize what I learned in a way it could be taught in ten weeks. During this process those disparate notes and personal experiences came into focus in a clear and logical way.

Six essential elements of a systematic belief system emerged—foundational truths to empower a successful healing ministry. Think of them as gates that open and close, prospering or hindering your ministry of healing. For many believers, one or more of these theological gates may be closed. Numerous books have been written on each, but my goal here is to keep them simple and straightforward, revealing essential doctrine for a robust ministry of healing. Through a change of thinking (a good definition of repentance), a powerful approach to divine healing will be opened to you. It really does matter what you believe.

I write about each of these six elements with the revelation and understanding I have come to know at this time. I am certain that these (and perhaps more) are foundational to a fruitful healing ministry, but the level of understanding of each is unlimited. If I were to write this book again in five years, undoubtedly there would be greater and deeper truths revealed.

When you became a Christian, you were born into an adventurous life, walking in the footsteps of Jesus … something that is exciting, fruitful, and risky! Expect to break out into a fresh new walk with God as you discover these six truths. God wants to do extraordinary things through you.

All six, in one way or another, flow from two short but powerful Scriptures:

> *"Then He called His twelve disciples together and gave them power and authority over all demons, and to cure diseases. He sent them to preach the kingdom of God and to heal the sick" (Luke 9:1-2).*
>
> *"For laying aside the commandment of God you hold the tradition of men ... making the word of God of no effect through your tradition which you have handed down. And many such things you do." (Mark 7:8, 13).*

After two chapters introducing this subject of divine healing, I will get right into it. Jesus told us the Holy Spirit will lead us into all truth, so as you read, read thoughtfully, carefully examining the Scriptures, seeking truth, and exposing lies you may believe that make the word of God of no effect.

All Hands On-Deck

It is often thought that the ministry of healing is for the special few, those with special gifts of healings or special anointing. Of course, the gifts of the Spirit listed in 1 Corinthians chapter twelve include the gifts of healing, miracles, and faith, but these ministries are for the whole body of Christ. God is raising up an army in these days, and I believe He is calling for all hands on-deck. Every believer qualifies to be God's ambassador and minister healing to the saved and lost alike through the power of the Holy Spirit and the word of God.

A brief word about the book cover, beautifully designed by my friend Gitit Ezagouri. She designed it using the theme of the ancient Japanese art of kintsugi. This is the skillful art of repairing broken pottery with gold. This motif is evocative of what God does with His children, taking the broken pieces of our lives, reshaping, and repairing them into something beautiful. This is especially true as His divine power performs signs, wonders, and miracles of healing and deliverance.

Introduction

Most people have a general idea of how the lock on their front door works. The key has its own unique shape, allowing only one key to open the lock. The ridges on the key are uniquely cut to match the lock. Inside the lock are vertical pins of different lengths. Only the correct key will align the pins so the tumbler will turn and unlock the door. If one pin fails to line up properly, the lock will not open. They all must be aligned perfectly to allow the tumbler to turn and release the lock.

This is the picture I have in mind to illustrate the purpose of this book. There are six vertical pins in the lock that must be aligned properly to turn the tumbler and unlock the door. *Healing Right Now* will give you the key, cut precisely to open the door to an effective ministry of healing. I will describe six aspects of a systematic theology that must be believed for healing to be released through you. This is a bold statement, I know. *It matters what you believe!* because what you believe releases faith and affects how you pray and minister. This is what Jesus was communicating in Mark 7:8, 13:

> *"For laying aside the commandment of God, you hold the tradition of men ... making the word of God of* ***no effect*** *through your tradition which you have handed down. And many such things you do" (emphasis mine).*

What the Pharisees believed directly affected what they did. Jesus confronted the religious leaders who nullified God's word by obeying their traditions instead of Scripture. The Bible commanded these men to honor their parents, including the giving of monetary support. The Pharisees, however, created a novel idea that sidestepped the biblical command—they called this money *Corban* which meant "dedicated to the temple." This, no doubt, was portrayed as being more spiritual than God's commandment. They turned a practical way of honoring parents into a religious tradition, canceling the commandment, and negating Scripture.

According to Jesus, this was an important matter with serious consequences, and by doing this, they made God's word ineffective. Other translations say nullify, make void, cancel, invalidate, or revoke the authority of the word. The principle Jesus drew attention to has broader applications. If we believe a false or incomplete interpretation of Scripture or misapply or misunderstand what it means about healing (or anything else), we cancel, nullify, and make it ineffective. Wrong beliefs cancel the power of the word of God, and we may not be aware of it! This is sobering, serious, and has wide-ranging repercussions.

Let's use this example to drive home the point. Suppose we look at three churches in your city. One church believes in cessationism—the miraculous gifts of the Holy Spirit as seen in the New Testament are no longer available to the church today. As a result, they neither pray for the sick nor expect to see divine healings in their church. The second church believes spiritual gifts are for today, and they believe God can heal—yes, He can do anything, if it is His will. This church prays for God to heal but sees disappointingly few results.

The third church not only believes God can heal today, but believe it is (always) His will. They have become skillful and pray in faith, expecting to see healings. The result? Many are healed and set free from sickness and bondages.

We have three churches who all love God and are trying to live godly lives and please Him. They have the same bible, the same Father, the same Jesus, and the same Holy Spirit, but experience very different results in the ministry of divine healing. Why? Very simply, the difference is what they believe. I say it again—it matters what you believe.

A central debate in the New Testament is *who is Jesus*, or stated more accurately, who do you *believe He is*? Factually, He is the Christ, the son of God, but what you believe is the crucial issue. The destiny of every individual is dependent on your answer to this question. The power of Jesus to heal also depends on what you believe. We see this on full display in Nazareth when Jesus returned home after performing miracles elsewhere. Scripture tells us He could do no mighty works there because of their unbelief. They believed Jesus was merely the son of Joseph who they knew as a boy growing up. To them, He was not the Son of God, the Jewish Messiah. This wrong belief negated Jesus' power and voided, made ineffective, that which was available to them.

Jesus is quoted in John 16:13: "However, when He, the Spirit of truth, has come, He will guide you into all truth; for He will not speak on His own authority, but whatever He hears He will speak; and He will tell you things to come." One of the Holy Spirit's ministries is to lead believers into all truth.

The Venn diagram below illustrates this visually. The large circle represents *all truth*—God's truth and the truth the Spirit wants to lead you into. The small circle represents the truth you and I know. As you can see, I have drawn this circle with part of it outside God's circle of truth. I think all would agree that we know only a very small fraction of *all truth* and part of what we think we know lies outside God's circle. This would represent lies we believe that may nullify, make void, cancel, invalidate, or revoke the power and authority of God's word. My goal is to enlarge your personal circle and move it inside God's circle, at least with respect to divine healing. When your circle is encompassed completely within God's circle, John 8:32 is fully empowered: "Then you will know the truth, and the truth will set you free."

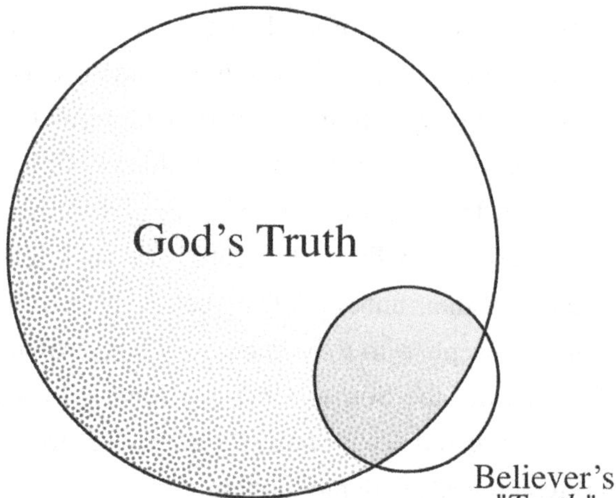

There is a growing momentum and interest in the ministry of healing in the body of Christ worldwide. This was launched over 2000 years ago when Jesus demonstrated and taught His disciples how to heal the sick. Since then, this ministry has experienced many twists and turns as the church has undergone various doctrinal swings and roundabouts over the centuries.

There is a hunger to see an authentic move of the Holy Spirit in our day—a demonstration of His power and presence as we witness the ministry of Jesus in greater fullness. In a sense, this is a restoration of the church's first love. What Jesus said to the church in Ephesus in Revelation chapter two is relevant to many churches of the 21st century, and many of us individually, me included. First, Jesus affirmed them with this:

> *"I know your works, your labor, your patience, and that you cannot bear those who are evil. And you have tested those who say they are apostles and are not, and have found them liars; and you have persevered and have patience, and have labored for My name's sake and have not become weary (Rev. 2:2-3).*

Following the affirmation came Jesus' loving rebuke:

> *Nevertheless I have this against you, that you have left your first love. Remember therefore from where you have fallen; repent and do the first works, or else I will come to you quickly and remove your lampstand from its place—unless you repent (Rev. 2:4-5).*

The church at Ephesus had fallen into a routine of "doing church," so to speak, persevering and enduring with its programs, works of service, keeping good doctrine, and serving God faithfully. This was all good and Jesus' affirmed them for faithfully keeping on keeping on. However, they had lost that fire seen in the book of Acts—the fire of first love for Jesus and the "first works" seen there—signs, wonders, boldness, and passion.

It is time to *get ready for better*! Our pastor here in Great Falls has given us this vision of getting ready for better. What is better? Better is first-love fire and power Jesus was motivating the church in Ephesus to return to.

If you are reading this book, you are probably one of those looking for more, hungering to see God's glory manifested more clearly and seeing the book of Acts come alive. There are untold multitudes of Christians who, for a lack of training, are frustrated by not seeing God's word and His promises fulfilled. If so, this book will *equip you to get ready for better!*

If you agree with and embrace these six elements of a systematic theology of healing, you will see the power of the Holy Spirit released through you in fresh new ways and will learn to minister healing effectively. I expect to convince you, through Scripture, that each of these is biblically sound and truth the Holy Spirit is leading you into.

So you will know where I am heading, here is a brief description of these essential factors. You will see these elements are interdependent, woven together into a tapestry, giving one overall picture of God's will and pointing toward an effective approach to a fruitful healing ministry.

God's true nature is seen in the life and ministry of His son, Jesus Christ. God is good. Jesus healed everyone who came to Him. Sickness is not a blessing nor one of the ways God disciplines His children. Everything begins with a right view of God. His will flows from a right understanding of His sovereignty and true nature.

Personal identity is an essential ingredient in a ministry of power, which I developed this thoroughly in my book *Stolen Identity*[1]. Many Christians believe they are servants of Christ, but little more. A successful healing ministry requires you to move beyond this. You need a personal revelation of being a son or daughter, an ambassador, a soldier, and a king, for it is within these identities you deal effectively with sickness, disease, and the devil. There is a battle between the kingdom of darkness and the kingdom of God. Healing and deliverance are ground zero in this war.

Healing is a finished work, accomplished as part of your redemption two thousand years ago. It flows from the cross. Yes, healing is in the atonement. Jesus said so! This means God's will is known and you do not have to pray "If it be Thy will …" God is *not* sovereignly choosing who to heal and who not to heal. His will is not the reason we see so few healed. We must look elsewhere for explanations. Jesus completed His part when He died on the cross and cried out "It is finished." We now partner with Holy Spirit to enforce the finished work of the cross.

Holy Spirit baptism and partnership, as seen in Acts is essential for an effective healing ministry. This is not an option in view of what Jesus instructed His disciples when He sent them out to heal the sick. The baptism of the Holy Spirit is a baptism for power and cannot be dismissed.

The believer's authority is a natural consequence of knowing your full identity in Christ. When a child of God begins to walk in his or her authority, they are following in the footsteps of the disciples. Jesus said, "Behold, I give you authority … over all the power of the enemy" (Lu. 10:19).

A kingdom of God viewpoint is a kingdom of power and love and is displayed when the sick are healed and those in bondage are set free. Most of us have limited ourselves to a church-centric worldview. Even though Jesus taught almost exclusively about the kingdom, few of us have been taught much about this.

As can be seen by some of these topics, I may be confronting, for many of my readers, some dearly held views. Other topics may be relatively new. Be ready to be challenged, as I was in my journey of seeking a greater measure of truth. I may step on a few toes and kill some sacred cows. If I do, it is in the vein of exposing beliefs that make the word of God of no effect. It is not personal! We are embarking on an adventure of purifying our belief system and removing unbelief, so it aligns with the pure word of Scripture.

One final thing I want to say here in the Introduction. There are hundreds of excellent books available on divine healing. This book is not meant to compete with them. Each of these six aspects of a systematic theology can and must be explored in more detail.

This book will be intentionally short (and sweet, I hope!). It will give you the big picture by illuminating the six essential areas where many Christians believe something wrong, which leads to ineffective prayer and ministry. There is a better way to pray. James 5:16 says it this way: "The effective, fervent prayer of a righteous man avails much." If there is an effective way to pray, then there is obviously ineffective ways to pray!

As seen in my acknowledgements, my wife and I have studied extensively under many world-class five-fold ministers on this subject. We stand on their shoulders. Barb and I have come a long way. We have been Spirit-filled believers from the start but were woefully ignorant and needed to be taught the word of God more fully.

Healing Right Now is aimed at equipping an army of God's people in a fruitful and powerful ministry of healing. It is also equally applicable if you personally need healing. Healing is your inheritance, as you will soon see. It is given to you as a grace benefit, a blessing flowing from Christ's finished work on the cross. It is part of the atonement. Receive it by faith.

May this book open your eyes and bring personal revelation to you. Revelation is a great blessing for us because it uncovers what the enemy has tried to cover over.

I have heard more than once from evangelical Christians something like this … "I don't *need* to see miracles in my life or in our church," even though they believe God still heals today. If this is you, read on. I think you will change your mind as you see the heart of the Father, His love for people, and His passion to bring in an end-time harvest. This ministry is at the heart of the plans and purposes of God. It is not an elective subject, but part of the core curriculum of Jesus' ministry.

Chapter 1

Why the Ministry of Healing Is Important

As I write this book, I feel compelled to finish writing and publishing quickly. It is both important and urgent. There are at least five solid reasons why this ministry is very important. The first and most important is the role of healing, signs, and wonders in God's plan for end-time evangelism.

With the events of the past few years, especially now as I am writing this chapter (the war between Israel and Hamas is intense), there is increased speculation in the church about the return of Christ. No one knows the time of course, but Matthew 24:14 says: "And this gospel of the kingdom will be preached in all the world as a witness to all the nations, and then the end will come." The gospel will be preached in all the world before the return of Christ.

Notice what gospel will be preached—the gospel of the kingdom. Jesus was intentional with His terminology here. He did not say the gospel of salvation, which is the primary gospel the church has been preaching in my lifetime. In chapter eight I will go deeper into the gospel of the kingdom but suffice it to say here, this gospel is a gospel of power, signs, and wonders. It was the gospel Jesus and the early church disciples preached.

> *"Then He called His twelve disciples together and gave them power and authority over all demons, and to cure diseases. He sent them to preach the kingdom of God and to heal the sick" (Luke 9:1-2).*
>
> *"And Jesus went about all Galilee, teaching in their synagogues, preaching the gospel of the kingdom, and healing all kinds of sickness and all kinds of disease among the people (Matthew 4:23).*
>
> *"But go rather to the lost sheep of the house of Israel. And as you go, preach, saying 'The kingdom of heaven is at hand.' Heal the sick, cleanse the lepers, raise the dead, cast out demons. Freely you have received, freely give" (Matthew 10:6-8).*
>
> *"And He said to them, 'Go into all the world and preach the gospel [of the kingdom] to every creature. He who believes and is baptized will be saved; but he who does not believe will be condemned. And these signs will follow those who believe: In My name they will cast out demons; they will speak with new tongues; they will take up serpents; and if they drink anything deadly, it will by no means hurt them; they will lay hands on the sick, and they will recover'" (Mark 16:15-18).*

God is on the move on planet Earth. He is up to something. He is looking for the church to partner with Him in a move of the Holy Spirit across the nations to bring in a great harvest. A gospel of salvation devoid of power will not suffice. This is vividly displayed by Paul's word in Romans 15:18-19. Gentiles were brought to God, convinced by the power of the Holy Spirit in signs and wonders. It was not just Paul's words, but his deeds as well.

> *"Yet I dare not boast about anything except what Christ has done through me, bringing the Gentiles to God by my message and by the way I worked among them. They were convinced by the power of miraculous signs and wonders and by the power of God's Spirit. In this way, I have fully presented the Good News of Christ from Jerusalem all the way to Illyricum" (NLT, my emphasis).*

We see great evil around us—an epidemic of darkness, drugs, and addictions of every sort; a weathering assault on traditional values has deceived and blinded millions. Widespread secularism has hardened the hearts of entire nations. Islam (and other religions) is growingly virulent. Yet we are called to go into all these nations to preach a gospel of power and salvation. Only a gospel of power will be able to bring in the harvest, set multitudes free of their bondages, and break the strongholds of unbelief.

I recently watched two videos that highlight this. In one was a well-known Christian apologist discussing the identity of Jesus and the evidence for the resurrection with an equally well-known Jewish news commentator. No matter how excellent the arguments were, the Jewish man remained unconvinced. The second video was of a brilliant young Christian debating two young Muslim men. Again, no matter how compelling the evidence, the two men remained unconvinced. As good as apologetics is, if the gospel remains in the arena of the intellect, most will remain unchanged. After watching these two videos, I was left to imagine what would have happened if the apologists had demonstrated the power of God by ministering healing to these three men.

This is why Paul wrote to the Corinthians, "And my speech and my preaching was not with enticing words of man's wisdom, but in demonstration of the Spirit and of power" (1 Cor. 2:4). Paul taught and debated with Greek philosophers in Athens, evidently to little effect. (Acts 17:16-34). He learned that effective evangelism includes more than the preaching of words and debating ideas and philosophies.

The first reason a ministry of power is important is signs and wonders draw the attention of multitudes. In the early chapters of Acts, Peter and John performed dramatic healings, crowds gathered, and a door was opened to preach the gospel. In Acts 3:6-9, Peter healed the lame man. Crowds came, Peter preached, and two thousand were saved. This upset the religious leaders, of course, resulting in interrogation and a stern warning to cease. Leaving the religious court, Peter and John found their companions and a passionate prayer meeting commenced. What was their prayer?

> *"Now, Lord, look on their threats, and grant to Your servants that with all boldness they may speak Your word, by stretching out Your hand to heal, and that signs and wonders may be done through the name of Your holy Servant Jesus."*
>
> *And when they had prayed, the place where they were assembled together was shaken; and they were all filled with the Holy Spirit, and they spoke the word of God with boldness" (Acts 4:29-31).*

This pattern repeats in Acts 5—more signs and wonders, more interrogation, prison and a miraculous escape—all leading to opportunities to preach. This is the gospel of the kingdom in action. When Spirit-filled followers of Christ heal the sick and cast out demons, the word gets around town making quite a stir—a *kerfuffle.* This opens the hearts of multitudes as they see a God of love and power in action.

For the second reason this ministry is essential, let's turn to the first miracle Jesus performed. The principle of first mention is often seen to reveal important aspects of any biblical topic. Jesus' first miracle was at the wedding in Cana where He turned the water into wine. John 2:11 describes it this way: "This beginning of signs Jesus did in Cana of Galilee and manifested His glory; and His disciples believed in Him." In a sense, this is the flip side of the coin. If power evangelism is the earthly side, then the glory of God is the heavenly side.

The miraculous brings glory to Jesus. Why? Because only He can do the miraculous. Every other god fails at this point, from Islam's Allah to Buddhism's Confucius. Every New Age idea falls by the wayside. God's very nature is miraculous, beginning when He created the heavens and the Earth. His glory is to be revealed through the church. Can we truthfully say His glory is shown through our typical church services? God is the same God and believers have the Spirit of Christ. Jesus deserves the glory due His name. As the church is trained and released in the ministry of healing, God's glory will be seen around the world again.

Thirdly, a ministry of healing displays not only God's miraculous power, but it reveals His true nature. It is a manifestation of His kindness, His mercy, His love, His patience, His peace. This is clearly seen in the life and ministry of Jesus. God's love is extravagant, over-the-top, beyond earthly experience or understanding. The Father's love should compel us as we see so many around us with broken lives, suffering with sickness, disease, and addictions. How can we settle for church as normal—inviting people to our meetings to hear a message or bible teaching, perhaps including an invitation for salvation, get them involved in the life of the church, and leave it at that? These church things are all good, but must not stop there. I trust you, my reader, will agree with me in this assessment, that our churches are filled with believers who are sick, diseased, depressed, and caught in cycles of defeat. Our compassion needs expression to heal and set the captives free. These two Scriptures are but a small sample of Jesus' heart:

> *"But when He saw the multitudes, He was moved with compassion for them, because they were weary and scattered, like sheep having no shepherd. Then He said to His disciples, 'The harvest truly is plentiful, but the laborers are few'" (Matthew 9:36-37).*
>
> *"Now a leper came to Him, imploring Him, kneeling down to Him and saying to Him, 'If You are willing, You can make me clean.' Then Jesus, moved with compassion, stretched out His hand and touched him, and said to him, 'I am willing; be cleansed'" (Mark 1:40-41).*

The church has excelled at feeding the poor, helping the homeless, and other works of compassion, but any secular organization can do the same. Only the church can heal the sick and set people free from demonic bondages. We need to minister to those in need in the power of the Holy Spirit.

Fourthly, the church needs to be strengthened in its faith. Paul writes something shocking in 1 Corinthians 2:1-5. He did not come to the Corinthians with excellence of speech or wisdom. He came in weakness, fear, and trembling. His preaching was not with persuasive words of human wisdom but "in the demonstration of the Spirit and of power, that your faith should not be in the wisdom of men but in the power of God."

This is quite a challenge to our modern western church. How many churches' faith is in the power of God—obviously referring to signs and wonders? What would Paul say if he walked into your church? This is not a criticism, just an assessment. Times of shaking are on the horizon and we, the body of Christ, need strong faith, not in our preaching and programs, but in the power of God.

The fifth reason: Although there are other reasons we could discuss, let me finish with an Old Testament passage that is personal to me—Judges 2:7, 10-12a. This passage describes what happened to Israel at the death of Joshua and the arising of another generation:

> *"So the people served the Lord all the days of Joshua, and all the days of the elders who outlived Joshua, who had seen all the great works of the Lord which He had done for Israel. When all that generation had been gathered to their fathers, another generation arose after them who did not know the Lord nor the work which He had done for Israel. Then the children of Israel did evil in the sight of the Lord, and served the Baals; and they forsook the LORD God of their fathers..."*

Read carefully to catch the importance of what happened. This caught my attention while pastoring in the UK. I took it to heart. My wife and I guided our church to became intentional in raising the next generation by turning our eyes and ears towards seeking the power of God. We prayed for the sick in our church and saw our fair share of healings. We set aside time at every service for testimonies of God's goodness and power. We also took advantage of every visiting missionary and asking every person we knew to sit at our dinner table and tell stories of miracles they had witnessed in Africa and elsewhere. We endeavored to raise a new generation who saw and encountered a God of power.

Many statistics tell us of young people who were brought up in church, then fell away from their faith as they grew up, moved out on their own, and went to university. It breaks our hearts. I ask myself, *what was their church experience? What was their view of God? What was their relationship with God? Was it limited to fun and games in the youth ministry or did they see miracles and witness the power of God up front and personal? Did they personally know a God of love and power?*

Our young people are being sent out into a world hostile to their faith and are being indoctrinated in every evil thing. I believe one of our greatest weapons against this plan of the enemy is for them to see and experience God's power on many fronts, especially to heal the sick.

Yes, I believe it is time for the church in our generation to rise up and once again press into the ministry of the kingdom of God, a kingdom of love, kindness, compassion, and power. This ministry of healing should not be taken lightly. If you have the attitude I mentioned at the end of the Introduction, *I don't need to see healings and miracles,* please reconsider. It is not about you! The world is crying out for a God of power to heal, deliver, and release from bondages. There is an advancing wave of the Holy Spirit in this hour. Carpe Diem! Let us seize the day!

Additional Scriptures: Ps. 103:8; Dan. 4:2-3, 17; Hos. 11:1-4; Joel 2:28; Micah 7:18-19; Hag. 2:6-7; Lu. 1:34-38, 46-55; Jn. 20:21-23; Acts 15:8-12, 28:8-9; 1 Cor. 2:1-5; Gal. 5:6; Eph. 1:16-20; 1 Thess. 1:5; Heb. 2:2-4; Rev. 2:1-5, 3:1-3, 3:14-22.

Questions to Consider:

1. Has this chapter challenged you in any way? How and why?
2. Can you add additional reasons the ministry of healing is important?
3. Consider how the Great Commission was taken to the lost world by Paul, the pioneer and most important evangelist of all time (Acts 14:3, 8-10, 16:16-18, 19:1-7, 11-12, 20:9-12, 28:3-10; 1 Cor. 2:4, 1 Thess. 1:5). Compare his methods with your experience and what you see today. Do you see a difference?
4. Consider the passing of the baton from your generation to the next—are you concerned? Is the next generation seeing God's power?

Chapter 2

Reasons to Believe God Heals Today and Wants You Well

This is a very important chapter. We must be convinced that it is God's will to heal today—right now! Without this assurance it is impossible to pray in faith, knowing with certainty you are ministering in God's will. Prayers of hope may seem nice and loving but offer little promise of fulfillment. Prayers of faith are powerful. Knowing God's will is the foundation of an effective healing ministry.

Every nation has its own currency by which its citizens engage in commerce. US dollars will not buy you anything in France. The currency of the kingdom of God is faith. It is through faith you receive from God. It is through faith you appropriate the spiritual blessings and covenantal promises given to you. First and foremost, you receive your salvation by faith (Eph. 2:8). This is the first step. In Ephesians 1:3 Paul writes: "Blessed be the God and Father of our Lord Jesus Christ, who has blessed us with every spiritual blessing in the heavenly places in Christ." Every blessing is received by faith. You receive the baptism of the Holy Spirit by faith. You receive your healing by faith. You minister healing to others by faith. Without faith it is impossible to please God (Heb. 11:6).

My personal observation is that many Christians have undervalued the importance of faith. The consequences are not insignificant. Countless believers are weak in faith, living subpar lives, and ignorant of the power and authority available to them. This has a direct and dramatic effect on the ministry of healing.

The word faith or faithfulness occurs over 300 times in the New Testament. The word believe appears over 250 times. Over and over Jesus says *go, your faith has made you well*, or something similar. Even a surface study of Jesus' healing ministry will reveal a direct linkage between faith and healing. The negative is also true. In Nazareth He could not do any mighty works because of their unbelief.

We may not fully know the process of healing or the timing, but we do know it is always His will to heal. Each of these seven reasons below deserves a full chapter or even its own book. The first two reasons will be developed more fully later in the book. As we go along I will provide recommended reading for further study.

Reason Number One: God's name and His nature define Him. This is revealed in both the Old Testament and the New Testament. Names are very important in biblical Hebrew. A name is the thing by which a person is known. It often describes the person's character and nature. Parents choose names for their children, but God chose His own name(s) to describe Himself more fully. One of those is first seen in Exodus 15:26, then described again in Exodus 23:25-26. This compound name is Jehovah Rapha, which means *The Lord my Healer.*

> *"If you diligently heed the voice of the Lord your God and do what is right in His sight, give ear to His commandments and keep all His statutes, I will put none of the diseases on you which I have brought on the Egyptians. For I am the Lord who heals you" (Jehovah Rapha; Ex. 15:26, emphasis mine).*
>
> *"So you shall serve the Lord your God, and He will bless your bread and your water. And I will take sickness away from the midst of you. No one shall suffer miscarriage or be barren in your land; I will fulfill the number of your days" (Ex. 23:25-26).*

"I am the Lord that heals you" is the present continuous tense in Hebrew. It is a continual process. God has not changed His nature. He is the same yesterday, today, and forever. There are other compound names of God. He is Jehovah Jireh (our Provider), Jehovah Nissi (our Banner), Jehovah Shalom (our Peace), Jehovah Raah (our Shepherd), Jehovah Tsidkenu (our Righteousness), and Jehovah Shammah (Ever present). He is each of these today, and He is still Jehovah Rapha, our Healer.

The New Testament expands and clarifies God's healing nature. Hebrews 1:3 and Colossians 1:15 tell us Jesus is the brightness of God's glory and the express image of God Himself. Jesus tells one of His disciples that if you have seen Me you have seen the Father (John 14:9). He also says, "The Father and I are one" (John 10:30). In John 14:7 Jesus says, "If you had known Me, you would have known My Father also; and from now on you know Him and have seen Him."

God's nature, Jehovah Rapha, is fully manifested in the person of His Son, Jesus Christ. Jesus' healing ministry is the outworking of the true nature of God. In other words, *like father like son*! And to cap it off, Jesus introduced to His disciples the deepest and most personal name of God, *Father*. As His sons and daughters, He wants us to know Him as Abba, Daddy. Every child deserves to know Father as He really is—He is good, all the time.

Reason Number Two: Healing is in the Atonement. Believing this is true has a dramatic impact on our faith for healing. If Christ died for our sicknesses as well as our sins, then every one of us can rest assured it is God's will for us to be healed and made well. As God desires that all would be saved (2 Pet. 3:9), He also desires that all would be healed. Scripture makes this abundantly clear—Isaiah 53 states prophetically that Jesus will atone for both sins and sicknesses. Jesus confirmed this interpretation of Isaiah 53 after healing Peter's mother-in-law in Matthew 8:14-17. It is then confirmed by Peter in 1 Peter 2:24.

> *Surely He has borne our griefs [lit. sicknesses]*
> *And carried our sorrows [lit. pains];*
> *Yet we esteemed Him stricken*
>
> *Smitten by God, and afflicted.*
> *But He was wounded for our transgressions,*
> *He was bruised for our iniquities;*
> *The chastisement for our peace was upon Him,*
> *And by His stripes we are healed (Is. 53:4-5).*

The word translated griefs in verse 4 is the Hebrew word *kholee* which means sickness. This word is used only for physical healing with one exception when it refers to the repairing of the temple, which was a physical restoration. It is not speaking of a spiritual healing. The New Revised Standard translation makes this clear: "Surely he has borne our infirmities and carried our diseases; yet we accounted him stricken, struck down by God, and afflicted." The New American Standard Bible: "However, it was our sicknesses that He Himself bore, and our pains that He carried …"

Jesus then removed any doubt as to its meaning in Matthew 8:16-17. Following His healing of Peter's mother-in-law the Bible says:

> *When evening had come, they brought to Him many who were demon-possessed. And He cast out the spirits with a word, and healed all who were sick, that it might be fulfilled which was spoken by Isaiah the prophet, saying: "He Himself took our infirmities, and bore our sicknesses" (emphasis mine).*

Jesus healed all who were physically sick as a fulfillment of Isaiah 53:4-5. This should convince everyone that the Isaiah passage on atonement includes physical healing. The greatest Bible scholar of all time, Jesus, interpreted it for us and removed all doubt.

In 1 Peter 2:24 it is once again confirmed: "…who Himself bore our sins in His own body on the tree, that we, having died to sins, might live for righteousness—by whose stripes you were healed." Notice that it describes healing in the past tense. The provision for our healing is just like the provision for salvation and all other benefits given to us—provision was made two thousand years ago! Derek Prince would often say it this way: *The sole basis of our healing and deliverance is the finished work of the cross.*

This has important implications for ministering healing. *We do not pray, asking God to do something He has already done!* He completed His part two thousand years ago. It is now our responsibility, in partnership with the Holy Spirit, to do as the disciples did—minister healing through the power and authority given to us. If you desire to study this further, I highly recommend a little book by Dr. T.J. McCrossan called Bodily Healing and The Atonement[1]. Dr. McCrossan was an eminent Greek and Hebrew scholar, and he goes into great detail answering all questions skeptics have asked over the years.

Reason Number Three: All sin and sickness is the result of Satan's work when he introduced sin into the world in Genesis chapter three. This follows directly from our previous reason. Sin and sickness are connected in the teaching and ministry of Jesus. In Hebrew thought, all sickness was thought to be the consequence of sin; when the root was dealt with (sin) so was the fruit (sickness and disease), because sickness and disease are a result of original sin. Healing is a manifestation of the righteousness of God. Sickness is to the body what sin is to the soul. Jesus' death, the shedding of His blood, is the one sacrifice for all time for all righteousness.

How did sickness enter the world? Romans 5:12 tells us: "Therefore, just as through one man [Adam] sin entered the world, and death through sin, and thus death spread to all men, because all sinned." Death (and sickness that leads to death) entered the world when Satan enticed Adam to sin.

This is good news for us because Jesus came to destroy the works of the devil! (1 John 3:8). Hebrews 2:14 says "… that through death He might destroy him who had the power of death, that is, the devil …" Jesus not only carried our sickness on the cross, He defeated Satan (and his works) who was the originator of this mess. He redeemed it all and then delegated power to His followers to enforce this victory. Jesus' commissioned His twelve disciples:

> *"Then He called His twelve disciples together and gave them power and authority over all demons, and to cure diseases. He sent them to preach the kingdom of God and to heal the sick (Lu. 9:1-2).*

Immediately following this commission, Jesus sent out seventy more disciples in the next chapter. Upon their return from their short-term mission, Jesus described what He saw occurring in the spiritual realm:

> *"Then the seventy returned with joy, saying, "Lord, even the demons are subject to us in Your name." And He said to them, "I saw Satan fall like lightning from heaven. Behold, I give you the authority to trample on serpents and scorpions, and over all the power of the enemy, and nothing shall by any means hurt you" (Luke 10:17-20).*

Do you see that? We have been given authority over all the power of the enemy! This includes sickness and disease. Again, this has important implications on how we pray and minister healing when we realize and utilize our authority as believers.

Reason Number Four: Jesus healed them all. In every case Jesus healed those who came to Him for healing and deliverance. He never turned anyone away. Sinners came to Him, Gentiles came to Him, religious leaders came to Him, men and women as well as boys and girls. He healed them all. This precedence is another convincing reason it is God's will to heal all who come to Him.

Luke 4:18-19 and Acts 10:38 give an overview of Jesus' purpose and calling:

> *"The Spirit of the Lord is upon Me, Because He has anointed Me to preach the gospel to the poor; He has sent Me to heal the brokenhearted, to proclaim liberty to the captives And recovery of sight to the blind, To set at liberty those who are oppressed; To proclaim the acceptable year of the Lord" (Lu. 4:18-19).*
>
> *"...how God anointed Jesus of Nazareth with the Holy Spirit and with power, who went about doing good and healing all who were oppressed by the devil, for God was with Him" (Acts. 10:38, emphasis mine).*

As you can see, the foundation of His purpose and calling was to bring physical and spiritual wholeness to all who would receive Him. Subsequently, Jesus passed the ministry baton to His disciples and then to all His followers as part of the Great Commission. Acts 5:12-16 describes how signs and wonders were done by the apostles. Multitudes of the sick and tormented souls came from surrounding cities "... and they were *all healed.*"

Paul, inspired by the Holy Spirit, informs us of nine gifts of the Holy Spirit in 1 Corinthians 12:4-11. Within this list are the gifts of healings, faith, and the working of miracles, all of which bear directly on divine healing. This passing of the baton from Jesus to His followers confirms it is (always) God's will to heal the sick and set captives free.

Reason Number Five: The Lord's Prayer is the best description of His will. In the Sermon on the Mount, Jesus included how not to pray—don't pray like the hypocrites looking for public exaltation but pray in private without using "vain repetitions." He then gave them the model prayer (Matt. 6:9-13) that begins: "Our Father in heaven, hallowed be Your name. Your kingdom come. Your will be done on earth as it is in heaven."

This is the best definition of the will of God found anywhere in Scripture. God's will is Earth should reflect heaven. Certainly, there is no sickness or disease in heaven. There are no demons in heaven. Jesus came to bring abundant life (Jn. 10:10), life that reflects heaven and is a manifestation of the kingdom of God.

Although Earth does not reflect heaven on a regular basis, it is, nevertheless, God's will (or His desire). Our lives—marriages, families, relationships, and callings reflect heaven when they are in accordance with His will. When sickness is present, God's kingdom is not ruling. However, when someone is healed, "His kingdom has come and His will is done." This is our calling as sons and daughters who carry on His ministry—to bring order out of disorder; to bring healing where there is sickness and disease. When the kingdom of God in us is released into a situation, Earth reflects heaven.

Reason Number Six: James 5:14-15 clearly teaches it. In the New Testament and in the context of the local church, the apostle James wrote:

> *"Is anyone among you sick? Let him call for the elders of the church, and let them pray over him, anointing him with oil in the name of the Lord. And the prayer of faith will save the sick, and the Lord will raise him up. And if he has committed sins, he will be forgiven."*

"Is there anyone among you sick" is an altar call for anybody in the local church to come forward and be anointed with oil and be healed. No one in the church was to be sick! Amazing to think about this possibility. This should get our hearts throbbing with excitement! One of the prevalent means of New Testament healing is the anointing with oil and praying in faith. James gives the expected result—total healing!

It is important to keep your eye out for patterns in Scripture that reveal key truths. One of the most important is seen in the pattern of divine healing throughout the Bible beginning in Exodus when God called Himself Jehovah Rapha through to this passage in James 5. You can be certain that it is God's will to heal.

Reason number seven: Christ's role as our great Shepherd requires the ministry of healing. Hebrews 13:20-21 says:

> *"Now may the God of peace who brought up our Lord Jesus from the dead, that <u>great Shepherd of the sheep</u>, through the blood of the everlasting covenant, make you complete in every good work to do His will, working in you what is well pleasing in His sight, through Jesus Christ, to whom be glory forever and ever. Amen" (emphasis mine).*

Once again, a name carries important significance. Every good shepherd loves his sheep and diligently takes care of them. Even more, Jesus is our *Great* Shepherd! David, who himself was an experienced shepherd, wrote in Psalm 23 "You anoint my head with oil." In ancient times the shepherd used oil to anoint the head and eyes of his sheep to heal them from the effect of flies and lice and other annoying enemies. Everything the shepherd did was for the health and protection of the sheep in his care because he loved them.

The prophetic passage in Isaiah 53 (for healing and salvation) uses the sheep metaphor in verses 6-7, as does 1 Peter 2:24-25. Our identity as sheep is a marvelous aspect of who we are in Christ, and it supports and defends Jesus as our healer. We need to see ourselves beyond the identity of servanthood into the width and depth and height of the other identity relationships with the Lord. This revelation will change your life forever. No longer will you wonder if He wants to heal you. No longer will you even consider praying "If it by thy will …" What shepherd would not want his sheep prospering and full of health?

I trust you will forever put behind you the question of God's will to heal, both you and others. If Satan whispers in your ear, "hath God said," do as Jesus did when he was tempting Him in the wilderness: "It is written."

Additional Scriptures: 1 Sam. 17:45; Psalm 23, 103:1-5; Prov. 4:20-23; Matt. 4:23-24, 7:9-11, 8:16, 12:15, 15:21-28; Lu. 1:20, 4:40-41, 6:17-19; John 5:14, 8:7-11; Acts 9:32-35; Rom. 8:1-11, 31-32; 2 Cor. 1:20; Col. 2:13-15; Titus 3:4-7; Heb. 2:14-15.

Questions to Consider:

1. Did this chapter expose any lies that you have believed, which makes the word of God ineffective? If

so, study the Scriptures in this chapter and do further research.

2. In Matthew 15:26 Jesus describes healing and deliverance as "the children's bread." Meditate on this and apply it to yourself.
3. Have you thought about the connection between sin and sickness? Meditate on this connection, seeing more deeply that the when Jesus' finished work on the cross defeated sin, it also dealt with sickness.
4. Read and study the following Scriptures. Select some of them to memorize and meditate on—to know His will and renew your mind: Ex. 15:26; Ps. 103:1-4; Ps. 107:20; Prov. 3:1-2; Prov. 4:20-22; Is. 53:4-5; Lu. 9:1-2; Jn. 10:10; Jn. 14:12; Acts 10:38; 1 Pet. 2:24; 3 Jn. 1:2.
5. If Jesus healed them all, why would He not heal you? Why would He not heal those to whom you minister healing?
6. Have you thought what it means to have an identity as a sheep in the fold of the Great Shepherd? Read Psalm 23 and contemplate on the blessing it is to be a sheep.

Chapter 3

God's True Nature

I will now begin an examination of the six aspects of a systematic theology of healing. In all my training, especially in the past seven years, I have identified six biblical concepts that are critical to an effective ministry of healing. Ask God for a revelation of these truths, as this solid foundation will put you on a fast track to a fruitful ministry. There is additional knowledge that can and must be added to what is written here, and I will provide suggestions for additional study.

We begin with the most important. What can be more foundational than knowing the true nature of God? A.W. Tozer has said "What comes into our minds when we think about God is the most important thing about us. The man who comes to a right belief about God is relieved of 10,000 temporal problems." (from Tozer's book *The Knowledge of the Holy*). Unfortunately, many Christians have a distorted view of God that directly affects the ministry of healing. In my view, this is due to a misapplication of His sovereignty. He is accused, by large portions in the body of Christ, of having His fingerprints on sickness and disease, tragedies, and premature deaths.

I want to begin this chapter with the subject of our personal in-Christ identity. In my book, *Stolen Identity,* I contend that many believers are stuck, identifying and living in the first and most basic personal identity—being a servant of Christ. This is an important identity, but it is only the starting place. Servants have masters and the servant/master relationship falls far short of seeing the true nature of God. We need a personal revelation of at least two others—our identity as sons and daughters and being part of the bride of Christ. Again, many Christians know about these doctrinally, but the relational transformation and intimacy that takes place with a revelation of these identities is powerful.

Unfortunately, many have not had good fathers, and none of us have had perfect ones. These experiences often get reflected in our relationship with our heavenly Father, even if unconsciously. We do not truly see how good He is and the depth of His love toward us. A revelation of the father heart of God brings a deep understanding of His love and is essential to a strong faith in His desire to see us healed and well. If the true nature of God were to be described in one word it would be love. God is love. "He who does not love does not know God, for God is love" (1 Jn. 4:8). The fruit of the Spirit in Galatians 5:22-23 expands our understanding of this foreign kind of love as it manifests in our lives: love, joy, peace patience, kindness, goodness, faithfulness, gentleness, and self-control. The foundation of the kingdom of God is the love of God, which is in direct opposition to the ways of this world. Jesus' life and teaching is the starting place to grasp the Father's love. He said all the law and the prophets can be summarized in this, to love the Lord your God with all your heart, soul, mind and strength, and your neighbor as yourself.

Jesus gave a wonderful parable to assist us in this, which is usually referred to as the parable of the prodigal son. I suggest a more appropriate title is the parable of the loving father. You may know the story well. The younger son asks for his inheritance early, before his father's death. Dad accommodates and off he goes. He soon finds himself in desperate circumstances and when he eventually comes to his senses, he turns around and returns home. What does his father do? He runs to meet him and smothers him with kisses. Not a rebuke or even a question that puts him on the spot. Papa fully restores him to the family, gives him a festive party along with a robe, a ring, and sandals. What kind of father does that; one filled with love in action. This is a demonstration of a new way of living, a kingdom lifestyle which is foreign to this world's system.

Jesus, in telling this story, gives us a powerful picture of God Himself. One of Jesus' primary ministry goals was to reveal God as a loving Father to His children. This may seem different than God as we see Him in the Old Testament. What happened at the cross released God to fully be Himself—His true nature. The sins of mankind were atoned for, and the New Covenant came into full bloom. That's why you see in Jesus the full revelation of the Father. God is good. He is love. He is on your side and not against you.

A common assumption is that one of the ways God disciplines His children is by putting sickness and disease upon them, striking them down in a bed of sickness. Scripture says something different. Paul writes this to Timothy:

> *All Scripture is given by inspiration of God, and is profitable for doctrine, for reproof, for correction, for instruction in righteousness, that the man of God may be complete, thoroughly equipped for every good work* (2 Tim. 3:16-17, emphasis mine).

In Ephesians 5:25-33 Paul gives instructions to husbands about loving their wives. He is to love her as Christ loves the church. How does Christ love the church? Verse 26-27 tells us: "…that He might sanctify and cleanse it [the church, His wife, His bride] *with the washing of water by the word*, that He might present it to Himself a glorious church not having sport or wrinkle or any such thing, but that is should be holy and without blemish" (emphasis mine). All would agree that God would not cause (proactively initiate) one of His children to sin. Jesus died to set us free from the power of sin. Jesus also died to carry away our sickness. Why would He put upon us something He died to take away?

God uses His word to reprove, correct, and instruct us. Think about it. Would any loving husband wish his wife to be sick and diseased? Of course not. This is a tradition of man, a belief not aligned with God's truth which has stolen faith from the church. It is easy to see why this thinking has come about. In Romans 8:28, a familiar passage to most, Paul writes that God causes "… all things to work together for good to those who love God …" Our Father is a master redeemer at using every trial, every work of the devil, every mistake we make, even our sins, to work for our good. Many people testify how God spoke to them or used their sickness for good. He is so good at this that He often gets the blame for causing sickness because of His ability to redeem pain or sickness. Again, this is not the word of God, but wrong thinking, making the word of God of no effect.

Let me ask you this question. In the parable of the loving father, can any blame be placed on the father for the problems his son ran into? His son had free will and the father did not stop him nor was he controlling the situation. This is a helpful picture giving a clearer understanding of God's sovereignty.

I am discussing sovereignty in this chapter because it is very important to our subject of divine healing. It is commonly believed God is always in control, controlling the events of your life, including sickness and disease. I want to challenge this idea. Before you get upset, let me explain.

If this is not properly understood and correctly applied, it negatively impacts any healing ministry in two ways. First, it leads to passivity. Instead of proactively partnering with God in ministry, we sit back and assume whatever the outcome, it must be God's will. If we are not proactive in partnership with the Holy Spirit in the ministry of healing, few, if any, will get healed. God does not use His sovereignty to heal unilaterally. It is not the way He runs His kingdom business!

A second negative is that God is blamed, if and when people do not get healed when a wrong emphasis on God's sovereignty is applied. Many conclude that it must not be His will to heal since He is sovereign. He evidently picks and chooses whom He heals, despite what the word of God tells us about His will to heal. The sovereignty of God is used as a rug under which we sweep everything we may not fully understand. As a result, many begin their prayers for healing saying "God, if it is your will to heal this person …" because we assume His sovereignty will rule in the situation. This is wrong and will diminish any possible fruit in praying for the sick.

God's will is revealed in Scripture and in the life and ministry of Jesus. Peter tells us in 2 Peter 1:2-3: "Grace and peace be multiplied to you in the knowledge of God and of Jesus our Lord, as *His divine power has given us all things that pertain to life and godliness*, through the knowledge of Him who called us by glory and virtue" (emphasis mine). If it is not life or godliness, it is not God!

Sovereignty is an immense subject and tackling it thoroughly here is preposterous. It would be arrogant if I implied I had all the answers. But if we keep to our subject of divine healing, we have a strong scriptural foundation, and I believe we will gain clarity. From what you have already read in this book about the atonement and about the life and ministry of Jesus, who was the perfect reflection of the Father, I want to declare again—God's fingerprints are not on sin, sickness, and disease. So, how do we square this with God's sovereignty?

The word sovereignty means supremacy. It does not mean God controls everything. If He did, we would blame him for the sin of Hitler, tragic accidents, cancer, and birth defects. I believe it is helpful to distinguish between God reigning and God ruling. These terms are often used interchangeably, but this brings confusion. The king of England, for example, reigns over the United Kingdom, but He does not rule. He has influence, but he does not rule (or control) in any meaningful way. God reigns over His domain (His kingdom) by virtue of being Creator. He is sovereign, He is supreme. This goes without saying. But He does not rule (control events) until or unless His will is being done. The Lord's prayer makes this clear. "Our Father in heaven, hallowed be Your name. Your kingdom come. Your will be done on earth as it is in heaven" (Matt. 6:9-10).

This makes two things clear. First, God's will is not always being done or He would not be asking us to pray it would! Secondly, His kingdom is ruling only when His will is being done. He reigns 100% of the time over everything, but He is ruling when His will is done. This happens in partnership with us—when we pray and when we use the power and authority He has delegated to us. The church often over emphasizes the authority of God and under emphasizes the authority of the believer. This is modeled for us when the disciples were sent out two by two to heal the sick. Sickness is not His will, but when they healed the sick His kingdom came into that situation, and His will was done. Let's review Scripture to drive home the point.

Jesus equipped and commissioned the disciples in Luke 9:1-2: "Then He called His twelve disciples together and gave them power and authority over all demons, and to cure diseases. He sent them to preach the kingdom of God and to heal the sick." Then in chapter ten seventy disciples returned having healed the sick and cast out demons. Jesus' response is enlightening: "And He said to them, 'I saw Satan fall like lightning from heaven. Behold, I give you the authority to trample on serpents and scorpions, and over all the power of the enemy, and nothing shall by any means hurt you'" (Lu. 10:18-19).

Satan's rule was overthrown when they used their authority and power to heal and deliver. This takes us back to Genesis one, two and three. God delegated to Adam and Eve the responsibility to manage matters here on planet Earth: "Then God blessed them, and God said to them, 'Be fruitful and multiply; fill the earth and subdue it; have dominion over the fish of the sea, over the birds of the air, and over every living thing that moves on the earth'" (Gen. 1:28). At the fall in Genesis three, they surrendered their responsibilities and Satan became, what the Bible calls, "the god of the world [age]" (2 Cor. 4:4). We see this confirmed when Satan tempted Jesus in the wilderness. "Again, the devil took Him up on an exceedingly high mountain and showed Him all the kingdoms of the world and their glory. And he said to Him, 'All these things I will give You if You will fall down and worship me'" (Matt. 4:8-9). It is confirmed a third time in John 14:30 as Jesus says, "I will no longer talk much with you for the *ruler of this world* is coming, and he has nothing in Me" (emphasis mine).

In Genesis three, Satan usurped God's delegated authority and responsibility given to Adam and Eve and began to rule, in a sense, in the affairs of men. Was God's sovereignty impacted? Yes and no. He is still sovereign in the sense of reigning overall, and He implemented His rescue plan (redemption through Christ's death and resurrection). Until Christ returns, there is a battle between two kingdoms. God rules in the affairs of men when we, as His sons and daughters, bride, ambassadors, kings and priests do our job of enforcing His victory on the cross. When we heal the sick, He rules. When we don't, He doesn't. We cannot attribute to God the sin, the sickness, and disease we see around us. He is not responsible in any way. If the forensic team from CSI Crime Scene Investigation was called to analyze those sick in the hospital, they would not find the fingerprints of God. He is not the author, the causer, nor the enabler of sickness and disease if sovereignty is properly understood.

My caution is this ... do not use ruling and reigning interchangeably, because to rule implies to control. God does not control everything. Yes, He intervenes (thank God!) in events, especially as we pray effectively. However, His primary plan at this time is in partnership with us as we, His sons and daughters, use our full identity to enforce His finished work on the cross—healing of the sick and setting free those in bondage.

(Parenthetically I want to add this. I do not at all mean God is on the sidelines of life and events on planet Earth. What I have said in no way diminishes His glory, power, majesty, or sovereignty. It simply acknowledges *His plan* to put all His enemies under His feet, and it embraces our responsibility in the purposes of God. He is active, involved, working all things toward His will. He is masterful and skillful as He elegantly weaves a beautiful tapestry in the lives of His sons and daughters and turns the tables on the devil working things for good. We see the end of the book and can know with certainty God is working in world events to bring about His will and all events will ultimately bring it about. *The above discussion is limited to and focused on divine healing.* God would never use His sovereignty contrary to His written word, and Scripture gives us clarity as to His will. If He were to invoke His power and authority in healing, it would be to heal—as seen in the life and ministry of Jesus, not to bring sickness and disease upon us).

God's true nature is seen in the parable of the father and in the face of Jesus Christ. Listen to Paul in 2 Corinthians 4:6: "For it is the God who commanded light to shine out of darkness, who has shone in our hearts to give the light of the knowledge of the glory of God in the face of Jesus Christ."

God's glory is seen not in sin and sickness but in the face of Jesus Christ, His life, and ministry. Our commission as His disciples is to follow in Jesus' footsteps, doing the works of the Father, and displaying His glory for all to see.

If this were a court case in which I was giving closing arguments to the jury defending God's true nature, I would close with this: Let us go back to the beginning and see God's heart (His true nature) towards His people Israel. This is seen clearly and succinctly stated in the only prayer in the Bible written by God Himself. It is found in Numbers 6:24-27 and is often called the Aaronic Blessing:

> *The LORD bless you, and keep you;*
>
> *The LORD make His face shine on you, and be gracious to you;*
>
> *The LORD lift up His countenance on you, and give you peace.*
>
> *"So they shall invoke My name on the sons of Israel, and I will bless them."*

The heart of God, like Jesus' parable, is to bless His children. God seals this truth in Deuteronomy 28, removing any possible doubt. God gives the children of Israel an exhaustive list of the blessings that will overtake them if they obey Him. This list goes for thirteen verses. Sickness and disease are nowhere to be found. Sickness is not a blessing and God's true nature is to bless his kids. You and I, as Gentiles, have been grafted into the fig tree (true Israel) with her covenants and promises (See Rom. 11:17). In Christ, we are justified, righteous 24/7 and fully eligible for these blessings.

Later in Deuteronomy 28, God warns Israel of the curses that will fall upon them for disobedience and idolatry. Guess what you find there—sickness, disease, inflammation, boils, fever, tumors, blindness, confusion, oppression—the list goes on and on.

When fully understood in the original Hebrew, the Aaronic Blessing is rich in meaning. Hebrew is an expressive language with many tributaries of meaning. Take for instance the final word of the blessing, *peace*. It means far more than we would understand from the English word. This is the Hebrew word, *shalom*.

I will quote from an expanded Hebrew definition of this from Warren Marcus's book entitled *The Priestly Prayer of the Blessing*[1]. From chapter eighteen: "One of the meanings of shalom is 'to make restitution.' … The heavenly Father restores sight to the blind, the ability to walk to the crippled, hearing to the deaf, and new clean skin to the diseased. God doesn't just heal a condition, He restores life, security, and hope to the brokenhearted! True *shalom* is to have every part of your life brought back to completeness and to wholeness!" This, my friend, is the heart and true nature of God.

In chapter 19 Marcus gives his amplified Hebrew-to-English translation. Our English Bibles read: "And give you *peace.*" His Hebrew-to-English reads this way:

> *"May YHWH (YeHoVaH, YaHWeH, your heavenly Father) set in place all you need to be whole and complete so you can walk in victory, moment by moment, by the power of the Holy Spirit. May He give you supernatural health, peace, welfare, safety, soundness, tranquility, prosperity, perfection, fullness, rest, and harmony, as well as the absence of agitation and discord."*

I rest my case before you, the jury.

To pursue the subject of this chapter more fully, I recommend two books. *God is Good, He's Better Than You Think*[2], by Bill Johnson. The second is *The Ture Nature of God*[3] by Andrew Wommack. These two books delve deep into the Scriptures and the nature of God as seen in the Old Testament as well as the New Testament.

Additional Scriptures: Ps. 34:8-10; Ps. 91, 138:1-3, 7-9; 139; 115:16; SS. 2:3-4; Jer. 31:3; Zeph. 3:17; Matt. 7:9-11; Jn. 3:16, 16:25-27, 17:25-26; Mk. 7:35-37, 11:22; Rom. 2:4, 5:1-8, 8:28, 31-32; Eph. 1:15-21, 5:25-28; Phil. 2:12-16; Heb. 11:6; Js. 1:2-4; 1 Jn. 3:1, 4:7-12, 16-19.

Questions to Consider:

1. What were you most challenged by in this chapter?
2. Have you believed God disciplined you by making you sick? In addition to 2 Tim. 3:17-17 and Eph. 5:25-27, read Rom. 2:4, Phil. 2:12-16, Prov. 6:23. Think through how Jesus' taught and disciplined His disciples. Now assess James 1:2-5, Rom. 5:1-8, and 8:28. Think it through.
3. Carefully read Paul's prayer in Ephesians 1:15-21. Ask the Lord for the "Spirit of wisdom and revelation in the knowledge of Him." Meditate on the three things Paul prays for to increase your understanding and receive a revelation.
4. If it is not correct to begin your prayers "Lord heal this person if it is your will," what would be a better approach? See Peter's example in Acts 3:6. Think of Jesus' examples.

5. Has this chapter challenged your view of God's sovereignty? Have your past views, if incorrect, caused the word of God to be of no effect? Think about why Jesus could do no mighty works in Nazareth and how this made the power of Jesus of little or no effect.

Chapter 4

Personal Identity

Personal identity is one of the most undervalued subjects in the life of a Christian. Few things have impacted my life more than a revelation of who I am in Christ—especially sonship. Receiving the Father's love as a son transformed my life, and brought me to a place of rest and deep relationship with God. How do you see yourself? Who are you? How does this affect your purpose and calling? Answers to these questions and more become pivotal in the context of a fruitful ministry of healing.

In the last chapter, I told how A.W. Tozer said the most important thing about a person is their view of God. It is interesting to note that C.S. Lewis disagrees: "I read in a periodical the other day that the fundamental thing is how we think of God. By God Himself, it is not! How God thinks of us is not only more important, but infinitely more important. Indeed, how we think of Him is of no importance except in so far as it is related to how He thinks of us"[1] (The Weight of Glory, 1941).

So, how does God see you? And more importantly, *do you see yourself as God sees you*? Is your view of yourself distorted by the twistedness of life—past or present, lies you believe, or a low-level view of Scripture? It makes a huge difference. Your answers to these questions determine, in large part, the course of your life. Despite good teaching and the truth of Scripture, I've found large swathes of the body of Christ push away the truth of God's love toward them and the treasures of blessings He has given. Many continue the treadmill of performance never fully receiving Father's love. In many ways they lead a life like the old school ground saying: *he loves me, he loves me not; he loves me, he loves me not*—all dependent on their self-perceived level of performance. It takes a personal revelation for these truths to touch your heart and transform your life.

In my 2022 book *Stolen Identity—Christian Who Are You?* I wrote about ten identities Christians possess because of Christ's death, burial, and resurrection. Four of these have a direct bearing on improving your skills as a minister of healing. Before I direct your attention to these, I need to lay a little groundwork.

The War on Identity

The importance of identity is self-evident to most people. It is not a small matter. One way to see the value of something is to understand the extent a thief would go to steal it from you. You don't need a home security system, a dog, and a guard at the front door to protect your rusted old bikes or broken rocking chair. They are of little value. However, if you have high-value treasures in your house, you will want to put security measures in place to protect them.

We see in the Gospels the primary battle Jesus faced regarded His identity. Who was this man from Nazareth? His opposition was on two levels—the human side and the demonic side. The religious leaders were relentless in battling against the notion He was the Jewish Messiah, the Son of God. They constantly confronted Him about who He was and where His authority came from (see Mk. 11:27-28). This continued to the final day of His life when Pilate asked Him, "Are you the king of the Jews" (Jn. 18:33)?

The devil is called the *adversary* (1 Pet. 5:8) and the *thief* (Jn. 10:10). We see him confronting Jesus in the wilderness. Twice he challenged Jesus' identity asking, "If you are the son of God …" (Lu. 4:3, 9). Now that Jesus is in heaven (His Spirit is of course with us and in us), we carry on His ministry until He returns. We are now the focus of identity attacks. If Satan can lie and deceive us at the levels of identity and authority, he will have blunted the power of the church, the body of Christ. Exposing lies and discovering truth is a primary purpose of this book. Knowing who you are, your identity, and the authority you've been given, is essential to His mission and your ministry. Receiving a fresh revelation of your personal identity, how God sees you and how you see yourself, will unlock immense potential in your ministry of healing.

One lie I want to highlight is illustrated by my youngest grandson Gabe, who is 9 months old. We were recently swimming with Gabe and his family. It was his first time, and he was giggly with excitement as he splashed in six inches of water. For him, it was an excitingly new adventure. Unfortunately, this is a picture of too many Christians I've encountered—those whose identity is simply "a sinner" saved by grace. The excitement of having your sins forgiven is wonderful but there is much more. You sin of course, but this is no longer your identity as a believer. You are the righteousness of God through faith (Rom. 3:22). You are holy and without blame, chosen, adopted, and accepted (Eph. 1:4-6). You are filled with the fullness of God (Eph. 3:19). You have been given the exceeding greatness of His power (Eph. 1:19). You have peace with God (Rom. 5:1). You are complete in Christ (Col. 2:10), and the list goes on. If you are stuck in simply being a sinner saved by grace, the Holy Spirit would love to take you into deeper waters. To be an effective minister of healing, you must walk out of past identities and embrace everything you have been given by grace.

Having said that, here are the four identities required for a powerful ministry of healing. In addition to *Stolen Identity*[2] I would like to recommend Bill Johnson's *When Heaven Invades Earth—A Practical Guide to a Life of Miracles*[3].

Sonship

I am using this word in a gender-neutral way, including both sons and daughters. In Ephesians 1:3 Paul writes that "God has blessed us with every spiritual blessing in heavenly places in Christ." Included in Paul's list is adoption—brought into Father's family and His circle of love. God is not satisfied with redeeming us to be mere servants who carry out His commands. He wants relationship, love, and partnership. For many this revelation unclogs the channel of God's acceptance and delight, enabling His love to flow unhindered in your life.

Many Christians push this away, feeling unworthy of sonship. This is Satan's big lie. This must be resisted. Jesus reveals God as Father. You are not worthy to be his son or daughter due to your good works but only because of Jesus' completed work of redemption. Many believers feel more comfortable keeping God at arm's length and satisfying themselves with servanthood. God is calling everyone into maturity and growth, into the deeper waters of the Christian life. This is an important first step—from servanthood to sonship. The Lord wants to work alongside us as He did with His son Jesus. He wants to share with us His heart, power, and authority in His kingdom business here on earth.

One of the ministries of the Holy Spirit in your life is to bring sonship into full bloom and unlock the flow of the Father's love into your daily life:

> *"For you did not receive the spirit of bondage again to fear, but you received the Spirit of adoption by whom we cry out, 'Abba, Father.' The Spirit Himself bears witness with our spirit that we are children of God, and if children, then heirs—heirs of God and joint heirs with Christ ..." (Rom. 8:15-17a).*

My friend, if you struggle with this, quit trying to figure it out! Receive it by faith.

Sonship is an essential aspect of an effective healing ministry for two reasons. First, Jesus was a son. His relationship with Abba was essential to His ministry. Jesus did what He saw His Father doing (Jn. 5:19-20). He had a close, personal, loving relationship with Father. He trusted His father and knew He was good, all the time. This is our model too.

Secondly, along with sonship comes the family's name, authority, and power. A master does not share this with his servants but does with his sons and daughters. As you have already read, the essence of the healing ministry is found in

Luke 9:1: "Then He [Jesus] called His twelve disciples together and gave them power and authority over all demons, and to cure diseases."

When the prodigal son returned home, his father bestowed upon him his best robe, a ring, and sandals. These represent the father's passionate love, authority, and honor. The robe showed the father's full acceptance back into the family. The ring was a symbol of authority—his father's delegated authority to do business on behalf of him, making decisions, and governing the father's realm. Sandals were a picture of inheritance, as ancient Hebrews used worn-out sandals to mark the boundaries of their property.[4]

Sonship is a matter of the heart. A child can be a son or daughter in the family tree but have the heart of an orphan—never feeling they belong or are loved. They live with a spirit of rejection, even though they are members of the family. God wants to overcome this with a personal revelation of a Father's love. It matters what your heart believes, for out of the heart flow the issues of life (Prov. 4:23).

A Christian who knows this and walks in the fullness of sonship is the devil's worst enemy. He stands tall and straight, walking in authority and power knowing he has the full backing of Father in carrying on the ministry of Jesus—preaching the gospel of the kingdom, healing the sick, and destroying the works of the devil.

There are many excellent books and resources on sonship. I have benefited greatly from all the resources of Fatherheart Ministries, led by James Jordan. His book *Sonship, A Journey Into Father's Heart*[5] is life-changing. I also recommend *Our True Identity: An Interpretation of Galatians* by Stephen Hill.[6]

Ambassador

Our Christian identity as ambassadors occurs twice in the New Testament.

> *"Now then, we are ambassadors for Christ, as though God were pleading through us: we implore you on Christ's behalf, be reconciled to God" (2 Cor. 5:20).*
>
> *"Pray also for me, that whenever I speak, words may be given me so that I will fearlessly make known the mystery of the gospel, for which I am an ambassador in chains. Pray that I may declare it fearlessly, as I should" (Eph. 6:19-20, NIV).*

Being appointed an ambassador is a great honor and comes with important responsibilities. From these two Scriptures we see our ambassadorial duties call us to make known the mysterious gospel of grace to reconcile unbelievers to Christ. Why is the gospel mysterious? It is other-worldly and completely contrary to the way of life in this world. Two kingdoms, two kings. A kingdom of light and a kingdom of darkness. The ambassadorial role becomes relevant when we understand and embrace a kingdom mindset. Most of us have been brought up in the church and have a church mindset—preaching, services, programs, kid's ministry, social events, outreaches, and building programs. A kingdom mindset brings us into a whole new ball game, a fresh and different way to see your Christian life and ministry.

The word kingdom occurs over 150 times in the New Testament. We are most familiar with its occurrence in the Lord's Prayer: "Your kingdom come your will be done on earth as it is in heaven." Jesus preached almost exclusively about the kingdom of God or as Matthew puts it, the kingdom of Heaven. His parables were parables of the kingdom. The kingdom of God is a kingdom of power. In 1 Corinthians 4:20 Paul tells us "For the kingdom of God is not in word but in power."

This is where healing and deliverance come into focus alongside our ambassadorial responsibilities. We are fully authorized and commissioned ambassadors representing our king to another kingdom. We let our light shine—living according to Jesus' New Testament patterns and demonstrating His power. His love is demonstrated not just in words, but in power. "And my speech and my preaching were not with persuasive words of human wisdom, but in demonstration of the Spirit and of power, that your faith should not be in the wisdom of men but in the power of God" (1 Cor. 2:4-5). We should settle for nothing less.

When we have a revelation of our identity as ambassadors we step beyond the life of a traditional Christian with a church mindset. We become commissioned representatives of the King of kings, which carries enormous responsibilities, far beyond going to church, listening to a sermon, and serving in a ministry.

Soldier

Not all Christians know that when you were born again you were born into a war—a war between the kingdom of darkness and the kingdom of light. This is a spiritual war that often manifests itself in the natural realm—your physical health and well-being.

The movie *War Room* is the inspiring story of Clara, the star of the show, who wins spiritual battles in her private prayer closet she called her war room. Clara is the epitome of a soldier in a spiritual war, winning her battles with a fighting spirit. The degree you embrace this identity, will in many ways, determine the course of your life! It will determine whether you live your Christian life on the back foot or the front foot; passive or proactive; defeated or victorious.

The soldier identity is seen throughout Scripture. Here are just two examples. Paul exhorts his spiritual son Timothy: "You therefore must endure hardship as a good soldier of Jesus Christ. No one engaged in warfare entangles himself with the affairs of this life, that he may please him who enlisted him as a soldier" (2 Tim. 2:3-4). Second is Paul's lengthy description in Ephesians six of the Christian as a Roman soldier in complete armor.

This war began prior to the Garden of Eden when God cast Lucifer and one third of the angels out of heaven. It continued in the garden when Satan deceived Eve. We see it in many places in the Old Testament (see for example Daniel 10:10-13). We see Satan confronting Jesus three times in the wilderness immediately after Jesus was baptized by John the Baptist. We see Jesus tell Peter "Get behind me Satan" in Matthew 16:23. Satan is clearly one of our enemies in this life, along with the world and our own flesh.

Most earthly wars have a frontline, where the battle is the most intense. The frontline in this spiritual war is where the kingdom of light confronts the kingdom of darkness. Jesus succinctly described the nature of this battle in John 10:10: "The thief does not come except to steal, to kill, and to destroy. I have come that you may have life, and that you may have it more abundantly." With John 10:10 in view, it takes little knowledge of the gospels to see the frontline, the clash of two kingdoms, as the healing and deliverance ministry of

Jesus. The two forces were face to face as Jesus healed the sick and set captives free from death and destruction.

Seventy disciples were sent by Jesus on an evangelistic mission announcing the kingdom and healing the sick (Lu. 10:9). When they returned with joy excited about their success, Jesus responded, "I saw Satan fall from heaven like lightening" (Lu. 10:18). Jesus won. Satan lost. Seventy disciples were partnering with Jesus to advance His kingdom. In Jesus personal ministry, we often see Him dealing with the enemy as part of healing those sick and in bondage.

John 10:10 lays bare the battle we are in. In vivid terms Jesus describes His mission—life, and the devil's—death. This identity as a soldier cannot be brushed aside and left to other people. The Scriptures are full of the promises of God for your life, but they do not come automatically. Why? You have an adversary whose goal is to steal from you, kill and destroy every good thing Jesus has accomplished for you. This is not a small matter for you and your family. It is life and death.

Every son or daughter should be equipping themselves to be skilled soldiers in spiritual warfare. Jesus has already won the victory over Satan, including sickness and disease, but we must enforce it.

Let us briefly examine three Scriptures:

> *"... having wiped out the handwriting of requirements that was against us, which was contrary to us. And He has taken it out of the way, having nailed it to the cross. Having disarmed principalities and powers, He made a public spectacle of them, triumphing over them in it" (Col. 2:14-15).*

> *"... that through death He [Jesus] might destroy him who had the power of death, that is, the devil ..." (Heb. 2:14).*

The most important fact to know in this spiritual war is that the finished work of Christ is the sole basis of your victory. At the cross the devil was stripped of his power and authority. If this is true, then the $64,000 question many Christians have is this: *If Jesus has already defeated the devil and won the victory on the cross, why is the spiritual war still going on? Why am I in a spiritual battle*?

The key understanding comes from our third Scripture, 1 John 3:8b: "For this purpose the Son of God was manifested, that He might destroy the works of the devil." The Greek word translated works is *ergon*. It means a work, task, business, employment. I like to describe it this way: Satan's business license has been destroyed. His *legal authority* to do business was revoked at the cross. As an illustration, let's say your favorite restaurant has posted somewhere on its premises a license from local authorities giving them permission and authority to operate. If they were to lose that license due to improper handling of food, they lose their legal right to be open. They can continue to operate unless someone in authority comes along and enforces the legal judgment against them.

This is a powerful picture of our spiritual enemy, Satan, the accuser of the brethren. At the cross his license to do business was cancelled. Jesus fulfilled the law and gave us His righteousness. Everything the devil does—every attack he mounts against you is illegal, without authorization, or lawful authority. Jesus took his authority to do business out of the way, having nailed it to the cross.

When a believer understands this and uses his or her authority, they have the power to overcome him and stop his attacks. When a believer knows he is righteous, holy, blameless, chosen, and justified, the devil has lost his ability to accuse, condemn, kill, steal, and destroy. Satan wants you to remain ignorant. He lies and deceives so you will never exercise your authority in Christ, for if you do, he is defeated.

This brings us back to Jesus' commission to His disciples in Luke 9:1 when He "gave them power and authority over all demons and to cure diseases." To be an effective and fruitful minister of healing and deliverance to those in need, you must embrace your full identity in Christ as sons and daughters, ambassadors of the kingdom of God, and a soldier equipped with powerful spiritual weapons.

King

To understand this identity, we must go back to the garden of Eden when God first told us He made mankind in His image, male and female. He then instructed Adam and Eve, "Be fruitful and multiply; fill the earth and subdue it; have dominion over the fish of the sea, over the birds of the air, and over every living thing that moves on the earth" (Gen.1:28). This is the first picture of God partnering with humankind to subdue and have dominion (rule, manage, prevail) over the earth. This is confirmed in Psalm 8:5-6: "For You have made him a little lower than the angels, and You have crowned him with glory and honor. You have made him to have dominion over the works of Your hands; You have put all things under his feet."

This position of authority was soon lost to Satan when the fall happened in Genesis three, when Satan became the god of this age (2 Cor. 4:4). Jesus came to restore matters in partnership with His sons and daughters, taking back Satan's authority, and once again ruling.

After His resurrection, Christ was seated at the right hand of the Father in heaven (Rom. 8:34). Paul then describes how we have been raised with Him and seated with Him in heavenly places (Eph. 2:6). Again, a picture of ruling with Christ, due to our spiritual position in Him.

The kingly role is a role of action on our part as we begin to exercise our authority as son and daughters, ambassadors, soldiers, and *kings* seated in heavenly places. Kings rule and it is in this identity that we co-labor with Jesus bringing matters that are out of order (sickness and disease) into order (healing and health). This is best understood when we understand the Hebrew concept of *kingdom* ("Your kingdom come, Your will be done …". In Hebrew, kingdom is action. It is God ruling in the affairs of men. Kingdom is also the demonstration of God's rule through miracles, signs, and wonders. Wherever the power of God is demonstrated there is His kingdom.

Identity is immensely important to the ministry of healing. When fully grasped, you will begin to walk in faith and confidence, exercising your spiritual authority. You have been given everything necessary to receive the baton of our generation and continue the ministry of Jesus, fulfilling the great commission. It is time to stop being a spectator and get on the playing field!

Additional Scriptures: Judges 6:11-15; Ps. 115:16; Matt. 11:11, 16:13-16; Lu. 2:49; Jn. 15:15, 20:16-17; Rom. 4:1-6, 8:14-17, 29-30; 2 Cor. 3:18, 10:3-5; Eph. 1:3-12, 4:20-24; 1 Tim. 1:18; 2 Pet. 1:2-4; Rev. 1:4-6, 5:9-10.

Questions to Consider:

1. What are the most important truths you have discovered in this chapter? Be specific. How can you apply them to your life?
2. Carefully read 1 Timothy 1:18 and discuss how a prophetic word becomes a spiritual weapon. Then discuss how a Scripture, a promise of God, can be used to win victories.
3. 1 John 4:17 says, "Love has been perfected among us in this: that we have boldness in the day of judgment; because *as He is so are we in this world*." Meditate on this statement and apply it personally. How does this affect how you see yourself?
4. One of the most potent illustrations of the power of identity is found in Numbers 13, the story of the twelve spies sent into Canaan to spy out the land. Read this chapter and see how identity led to Israel's great failure. Read all the way to verse 33 to see the punch line.

Chapter 5

Healing is a Finished Work

"It is finished." Three words. Darkness covered the whole land from noon to 3:00 pm Jerusalem time. A great earthquake shook that area, and bodies of the saints of old arose from the dead and appeared to many in Jerusalem. The veil in the Temple was torn from top to bottom, and access into the holiness of God was opened to all. These are the most profound, sweetest three words ever spoken on planet Earth. They hold more power and more significance than most can comprehend. They open a door into more blessings than we will ever know. They demonstrate the love of God like no others.

The Passover Lamb was slain, one time, for all time. The precious blood of the Perfect Lamb was placed over our lives. The sins of the whole world were atoned for. Redemption took place as the price was paid for us to be purchased out of the slave market of sin and bondage. Satan was defeated. The power of sin was broken, and Jesus' stripes, His broken body made total provision for our physical healing.

Apostle Peter captured, as well as any man ever could, the essence of this in one sentence:

> *"Grace and peace be multiplied to you in the knowledge of God and of Jesus our Lord, as His divine power has given to us all things that pertain to life and godliness, through the knowledge of Him who called us by glory and virtue, by which have been given to us exceedingly great and precious promises, that through these you may be partakers of the divine nature, having escaped the corruption that is in the world through lust" (2 Pet. 1:2-4, emphasis mine).*

Apostle John adds more insight to the immensity of this Passover event by saying, "For this purpose the Son of God was manifested, that He might destroy the works of the devil" (1 Jn 4:8). When it was finished, the devil's authority on planet Earth had been recaptured.

Apostle Paul could not contain himself in writing my favorite chapter in the bible, Ephesians one. Every blessing Paul described emanates from these final three words of Jesus—"It is finished." Paul begins the meat of this chapter in verse 3 by saying "Blessed be the God and Father of our Lord Jesus Christ, *who has blessed us* with every spiritual blessing in heavenly places in Christ ..." (emphasis mine). By my count he described 27 spiritual blessings in the first three chapters of Ephesians alone! Notice that Paul said "who has blessed us"—past tense.

Peter, in 1 Peter 2:23, described Jesus' death on the cross and then in verse 24 writes, "... who Himself bore our sins in His own body on the cross, that we, having died to sins, might live for righteousness—by whose stripes *you were healed*" (emphasis mine). Again, notice the past tense.

The work of redemption and atonement prophesied by Isaiah in chapter fifty-three and the blessings that flow from the event punctuated by three words "it is finished" occurred two thousand years ago. Past tense. Every blessing is ready and waiting for every child of God to receive by faith and not by works. It is on deposit in a bank account with your name on it. This is called grace—the *other worldly* love of God in action. "But God demonstrates His own love toward us, in that while we were still sinners, Christ died for us" (Rom. 5:8).

As I wrote in chapter two, healing is in the atonement. It is contained in these powerful words, "It is finished." Healing is part of the finished work of Christ. John the apostle describes this man Jesus as the Word, the *logos*[1] of God: "In the beginning was the Word, and the Word was with God, and the Word was God." The Psalmist said, "He sent His word and healed them, and delivered them from their destructions" (Ps. 107:20). This *word* became the man Christ Jesus: "And the Word became flesh and dwelt among us, and we beheld His glory, the glory as of the only begotten of the Father, full of grace and truth" (Jn. 1:14). This word became the Word and was sent to heal us.

No longer should we routinely pray, "God, if it is your will, please heal this person." First, it is His will, and second, He has already made total provision for healing when He said, "It is finished." His healing work is finished. Jesus is now looking for partners to continue His ministry with the power and authority He gave His followers. Jesus said, "It is to your advantage that I go away..." (Jn. 16:7). He was speaking of sending the Holy Spirit at Pentecost to baptize the disciples with power. No, we do not ask Him to heal someone, nor do we ask Him to deal with the devil and the kingdom of darkness. We use our authority to enforce the victory He won on the cross two thousand years ago.

This brings us to our next subject, the authority of the believer.

Additional Scriptures: 1 Cor. 11:23-26; Lu. 22:14-18; Rom. 3:21-28, 6:1-14; Eph. 1:22-23; Heb. 2:9-18, 10:12-14; 1 Pet. 2:24.

Questions to Consider:

1. Think through the communion service. The wine represents Jesus' blood. What did that obtain for us? The bread represents Jesus' stripped, broken body. What did that obtain for us?[2]
2. Read carefully Ephesians one. Meditate on the blessings that flow from "It is finished." Personalize Paul's prayer in verses 15-21.
3. Read Paul's prayer in Ephesians 3:14-21. Can you see how this prayer flows from Jesus' finished work on the cross? Notice especially verse 20 and the partnership required for God to do more than you can ask or think. Can you accept that *you* are His partner?
4. 2 Corinthians 5:21 is known as the "exchange at the cross" ... our sins for His righteousness. Change the word sin for sickness and see what you think.
5. Read Isaiah 55:10-11. Apply this Old Testament passage to the Word made flesh. How did Isaiah capture the essence of "It is finished"?

Chapter 6

Holy Spirit Power and Partnership

Some years ago, I was studying in the book of Matthew, and I came to chapter twelve, which was the climax in Jesus' ever-present debate with the religious leaders. Jesus had just healed a man with a withered hand on the Sabbath followed by healing and delivering a man who was demonized, blind, and mute. The Pharisees attributed Jesus' power to Satan (Matt. 12:24). He taught them about a kingdom being divided against itself, refuting their claims vigorously. He warned them about speaking against the Holy Spirit, calling what they did "blasphemy" against the Spirit.

As I finished studying this passage, I heard in my heart a quiet but clear word: "The church is no better." I knew the Lord was not saying to me the church was guilty of blasphemy (like the Pharisees) but was guilty of rejecting the Holy Spirit. This was a wakeup call for me and gave me a strong desire to know the Spirit more deeply and yield to Him more fully. A.W. Tozer, in his book *The Divine Conquest* wrote a chapter called *The Forgotten One*. This was his observation of the church's attitude and practice toward the Holy Spirit in the

1950's. In some quarters of the body of Christ I think this is still a valid observation—the Holy Spirit is in the doctrine of the church but not in her practice.

This idea is not simply a modern-day phenomenon but harkens back to Paul's letter to the church at Corinth. In 1 Corinthians 12:1 Paul exhorted the church against *ignorance* of the gifts of the Holy Spirit. He then listed the nine gifts of the Spirit: a word of wisdom, a word of knowledge, faith, gifts of healings, working of miracles, prophecy, discerning of spirits, tongues, and interpretation of tongues. Ignorance began early in church history. The Greek word used here for ignorance sometimes includes a *willful ignorance*. There has been a consistent and ever-present war against the person and ministry of the Holy Spirit. This may explain, in large part, why the ministry of healing has floundered.

Holy Spirit Power

For this ministry to flourish, there must be an embracing of the power of the Holy Spirit. This is non-negotiable. He is to be at the center of our Christian lives. Jesus put it this way in John 16:7: "Nevertheless I tell you the truth. It is to your advantage that I go away; for if I do not go away, the Helper will not come to you; but if I depart, I will send Him to you." What a stunning statement to His disciples who had been His close companions for three-and one-half years. As these men and women embarked on a new season in their lives, the Spirit would be better for them than Jesus in the flesh. Ponder that!

After Jesus' resurrection, and just prior to His ascension the Bible tells us this:

"And being assembled together with them, He commanded them not to depart from Jerusalem, but to wait for the Promise of the Father, "which," He said, 'you have heard from Me; for John truly baptized with water, but you shall be baptized with the Holy Spirit not many days from now.' But you shall receive power when the Holy Spirit has come upon you; and you shall be witnesses to Me in Jerusalem, and in all Judea and Samaria, and to the end of the earth" (Acts 1:4, 5, 8, emphasis mine).

The word *power* comes from the Greek word *dunamis*, which means power, might, strength, ability, explosive, dynamic, mighty works, and miraculous power. As you probably know, our English word dynamite is derived from this word. This is the spiritual power to raise the dead, heal the sick, and cast out demons. An encounter with the power of God changes a person forever.

When Solomon finished the construction of the temple something similar happened. We read in 2 Chronicles 7:1-2: "When Solomon had finished praying, fire came down from heaven and consumed the burnt offering and the sacrifices; and the glory of the Lord filled the temple. And the priests could not enter the house of the Lord, because the glory of the Lord had filled the Lord's house." This is an Old Testament picture of a New Testament reality, as believers are God's temples. A beautiful picture of what happened at Pentecost as tongues of fire rested upon the disciples as they were filled with the power and glory of the Holy Spirit.

Let's return to Luke 9:1: "Then He called His twelve disciples together and gave them power and authority over all demons, and to cure diseases." The power given here was the power of the baptism of the Holy Spirit—power to carry on the ministry of Jesus and power to live victorious Christian lives. This was central to His ministry as seen in Acts 10:38: "How God anointed Jesus of Nazareth with the Holy Spirit and with power, who went about doing good and healing all who were oppressed by the devil, for God was with Him." If Jesus needed this power, if His disciples needed this power, then how can anyone assume it is unavailable or optional for us today?

I propose there are three lies, in context of this chapter, that make the word of God ineffective in Christian circles today.

First, the baptism of the Holy Spirit. For some reason, it is controversial, caught up in doctrinal disputes that have sidelined an essential ingredient in seeing the powerful ministry of Jesus flourish once again. Without this, in my view, we will not see God receive the glory due His name nor the gospel taken effectively to a lost world. Some say this is not for the church today. My question is simply this—where do you see this in the word of God, and why have hundreds of millions of Christians alive today received it? Why are huge portions of the worldwide church operating in the gifts of the Sprit and seeing signs and wonders? This power was necessary for Jesus, for His disciples, and it is necessary for us also.

The second lie is this—because many believe they do not *feel* the power of God; therefore, they must not have it. The answer to this lies in the fact that, as reborn believers, we are three-part beings—spirit, soul, and body. We use our five senses (see, hear, feel, taste, and smell) to inform us about our body and soul. This is a wonderful God-designed feedback system. However, our spirit-man is different. When we were born again, our spirit was made new. This Holy Spirit power we have resides in our spirit. Paul prays in Ephesians 1:19, "...and what is the exceeding greatness of His power toward us who believe, according to the working of His mighty power ..." and again in Ephesians 3:19 "... that you may be filled with the fullness of God."

This empowerment and these blessings reside in our spirit. Our five senses do not have the ability to sense what is going on in our spirit. So, how do we know we have this power? How do we know we are filled with the fullness of God? Scripture tells us! We receive them by faith and are released when we act upon them. You may not feel powerful, but you are filled with the fullness of God. You receive it by faith and release it by faith. Yes, there are times when you may sense the Holy Spirit's anointing, or you may feel heat in your hands, but that is not necessary. You are the temple of the Holy Spirit, and as such you cannot limit or confine His presence and power to one part of your being. How you feel is not the measuring stick.

The process of sanctification (discipleship) is, in large part, making our soul (mind, will, and emotions) aware of the riches that reside in our spirit. How does this happen? Scripture tells us that we are transformed by the renewing of our mind (Rom. 12:2) so that our thinking aligns with God's word. This is one of the goals of this book.

The third lie is how many Christians believe it is all up to God. They are ignorant of God's plan of partnership with His sons and daughters. I often hear something like this: *God is all powerful, and He can do anything*. This is true. However, it often springs from a viewpoint of waiting for God to move while the Christian hangs on, waiting for something good to happen, all the while believing this is virtue. This is wrong! While we wait for God to act, He is waiting for us to act—to use our power and authority to enforce the victories Jesus wrought on the cross. Satan is a defeated foe (Col. 1:13-15, 1 Jn. 3:8, Heb. 2:14-15).

Healing has already been provided. Many Christians live passively, coping with problems, including sickness, rather than using their faith and "the weapons of their warfare" (2 Cor. 10:3-5) to cultivate a life of victory. We are in partnership with God to extend His kingdom rule in our lives, families, cities, and nation.

There is another aspect of power that is often overlooked—the power of love. An encounter with the power of God's love is life transforming. It heals the total person—spirit, soul, and body. 1 John 4:18 says, "There is no fear in love; but perfect love casts out fear, because fear involves torment." Love heals the inner man, the mind, the will, and the emotions. This, in itself, can lead to healing of the body. There are many sicknesses and diseases that have their roots in the soul. A personal revelation of the love of God can destroy rejection, fear, anxiety, depression, even mental illness. I strongly recommend Dr. Henry W. Wright's book *Exposing the Spiritual Roots of Disease.*[1] Dr. Wright has been a pioneer in the spirit-soul-body connection.

For me personally, my salvation experience included a dramatic encounter with the power of God's love. When I surrendered and invited Him into my life, I was regenerated by the washing of the love of God. Every part of my being was transformed in five minutes. I experienced an immediate filling of all nine fruits of the Holy Spirit ... love, joy, peace, patience, kindness, goodness, faithfulness, gentleness, and self-control. This was a power-encounter with the Spirit of God, and my life was changed forever. Although it is not overtly described in Scripture, I cannot help but believe when Jesus healed all who came to Him, they felt His love being poured into their bodies and souls. God is love: Father, Son, and Holy Spirit. As we minister healing to those in need, it is most effective when the love of God is part of the package.

Holy Spirit Partnership

From the beginning, God began a plan of partnership with humankind. He delegated to Adam and Eve responsibility and authority to cultivate the garden and rule the Earth, "… having dominion over the fish of the sea, over the birds of the air, and over every living thing that moves on the earth" (Gen. 1:28). God chose to rule the Earth in partnership with His children.

Moving into the New Testament, one of Jesus' primary missions was to reveal to His people that God was their Father. What a stunning revelation. In His life and ministry Jesus, the Son, worked in partnership with Father. In John 5:19-20 Jesus revealed that he only did what He saw the Father doing.

Jesus spent 3.5 years training and discipling His men to carry on the ministry in His absence. Jesus made a startling statement in John 14:12: "Most assuredly, I say to you, he who believes in Me, the works that I do he will do also; and greater works than these he will do, because I go to My Father." Jesus was speaking here of the coming of Pentecost and the disciples' Holy Spirit baptism—all in partnership with the Spirit of God. This partnership runs throughout the New Testament.

Let's look at Ephesians 3:20-21, which clearly demonstrates the plan of partnership. Here, at the conclusion of Paul's powerful prayer, which began in verse 14, he says this: "Now to Him who is able to do exceedingly abundantly above all that we ask or think, *according to the power that works in us*, to Him be glory in the church by Christ Jesus to all generations, forever and ever. Amen" (emphasis mine). Two observations are important.

Yes, God is all-powerful and can do exceedingly abundantly above all that we ask or think, but He does them through us, His sons and daughters! In the Old Testament, God worked through prophets, kings, and priests. He delivered the Israelites from slavery in Egypt through Moses. Elijah prayed it would not rain for three years, and it did not rain. Then he prayed it would rain, and it rained. (Js. 5:17-18). This partnership continued in the New Testament. It was time for the gospel to go to the Gentiles, but He did not do it alone (sovereignly). He gave a vision to Peter and sent an angel to Cornelius in response to his prayers. They each obeyed and the rest is history. In Acts three, Peter used his power and authority to command the lame man, "In the name of Jesus Christ of Nazareth, rise up and walk."

Partnership with Holy Spirit is the essence of the healing ministry. His disciples have been given power, authority, and the command to go heal the sick and cast out demons (the Great Commission in Mark 16:15-20). We don't wait for God to sovereignly do something when He is waiting on us! We don't ask Him to heal somebody when He has commanded us to heal them!

"Everything the Father has is invested in the Son. And all the wealth of the Father and the Son is administered by the

Holy Spirit. The Spirit is the steward, the keeper of the storehouse. It will be to our benefit to make friends with Him! Let us be open to Him as He teaches us how to receive from that storehouse."[2]

Each person you pray for is unique. It is important to be listening to the Spirit, allowing Him to prompt and direct you in the specifics of ministry. He may give you questions to ask the person which open the door to freedom. Recently my wife and I were ministering to a woman who had trauma in her past. We sensed this was key to her healing journey. We invited the Holy Spirit into our time of ministry and asked Him to remind her of the most important (high octane) events in her past. As we quietly waited, the Holy Spirit opened just the right doors for her, which led to a powerful and fruitful time of ministry.

You may remember the story of Jesus in Luke five when He spoke to Simon Peter "Launch out into the deep and let down your nets for a catch" (Lu. 5:4). After protesting briefly, Peter obeyed. He caught such a large catch he had to call for another boat to help with all the fish. The greatest catch of fish is in deep waters. For greater fruitfulness in your life, you too must launch out into the deeper waters of the Spirit. Allow Him to baptize you with power, boldness, fellowship, and intimacy. Fruitful ministry of healing flows through a relationship with Holy Spirit.

Acts 19:11 tells us God worked unusual miracles by the hands of Paul. Miracles were normal in the first century church, but some were unusual. Is it not time we begin to say miracles are normal once again in the 21st century church?

Additional Scriptures:

Ex. 31:1-5; Joel 2:28; Ps. 27:4; Matt. 3:16, 12:28, 16:18-19; Luke 1:34-37, 41, 4:1, 18-19; Jn. 3:4-8, 14:10, 16-26, 17:26; Acts 1:16, 6:5-8, 7:51, 8:5-25, 29, 10:44-46, 13:52; Rom. 5:17, 8:11, 14:17, 15:18-19; 1 Cor. 2:4-5, 10-16; 2 Cor. 13:14; Gal. 3:5; Eph. 1:16-17, 6:17; Heb. 10:13; Js. 4:4-5; 2 Pet. 1:2-4.

Questions to Consider:

1. What is the most important thing you have learned in this chapter? Were any lies exposed?
2. What is your relationship with the Holy Spirit? Is He your priority? Is He your partner in life? What can you do to cultivate a deeper communion with the Spirt of God? (See James 4:4-5).
3. In 1 Corinthians 12:1, Paul tells the Corinthians not to be ignorant of spiritual gifts. Are you? In 1 Corinthians 14:1, Paul tells us to desire spiritual gifts, especially that we may prophecy. Consider a season of prayer asking for spiritual gifts.
4. Read carefully Ephesians 1:17-21. Read it in various translations. How do you received this power? (see Gal. 3:5).
5. Read Hebrews 10:13 and think through how partnership with Holy Spirit is necessary for Jesus' enemies to be made His footstool.

Chapter 7

The Believer's Authority

English poet Thomas Gray coined the phrase "ignorance is bliss." This may be true sometimes, but not in the context of biblical truth. In my experience, a large percentage of Christians are ignorant of their authority in Christ. Ignorance of this important truth has diminished Christianity and negatively affected believer's lives in countless ways. I included myself in this majority until I met my friend Don Crum. Don began to teach and demonstrate what it means to use my Christ-given authority.

In 2002 Don arrived in the UK to minister in our church. He arrived amid London's biggest ever manhunt for a serial sex offender. Over many months, a rapist had been attacking victims in Southeast England. More than one hundred detectives from four police forces were assigned to Project Orb. They had no leads as the direction of his assaults was moving in our direction. Just before Don arrived, this man struck his ninth victim in a town only five miles from our church. Several members of our fellowship lived there.

I remember vividly how Don said to me, “Gary, this man has now come into your territory. He is operating within your area of responsibility and jurisdiction. It is as much the church’s responsibility as the police. You have spiritual and governmental authority over this evil.” This was a wakeup call! I wasn’t sure what would happen next.

On Sunday morning, Don led our church in a powerful prayer, declaring and exercising authority over the evil of this situation. He prayed three specific things: This man would not harm anyone else; he would be caught within one week, and he would be caught by a Christian police officer! After months of intense investigation and little to go on, this man was caught on the 8th day by a Christian officer! The local newspaper described the officer as an elder in his church. Co-incidence? Of course not. This demonstration of the believer’s authority woke me up and set me on a new course.

Let’s review our principal Scripture in the ministry of healing. Jesus commissioned His disciples: “Then He called His twelve disciples together and gave them power and authority over all demons, and to cure diseases. He sent them to preach the kingdom of God and to heal the sick” (Luke 9:1-2). A thorough understanding of these two verses can become a college-level course in healing. Let me explain. There are at least five important truths here:

1. The ministry of healing, as seen in Jesus’ life, was passed on to His followers and it continues as an integral part of the proclamation of the gospel of the kingdom. We are in partnership with Jesus (and Holy Spirit) to heal and set prisoners free.
2. To be successful, we must have power.
3. To be successful, we must have authority.

4. This ministry exercises authority over the work of Satan and his kingdom of darkness. Spiritual warfare is not optional.
5. This ministry is called to preach the gospel of the kingdom. When the sick are healed and the bound are freed, the kingdom is demonstrated.

Authority comes from the Greek word *exousia*. Strong's defines this as "authority, conferred power; delegated empowerment (authorization), operating in a designated jurisdiction." Authority is the *right* to rule or perform an activity; power is the *strength or force* needed to do so. Authority controls and releases power; power backs up and enforces authority.[1]

My friend, Don, taught me about authority using the illustration of a crowded intersection in an African town where he once lived. No traffic lights, heavy traffic, potential chaos. A police officer in a dark suit with white gloves mounted a box in the middle of the intersection and directed traffic with the authoritative movement of his arms and the blowing of his whistle. He used his authority to enforce the traffic laws. He did not have the strength or power to stop 5000-pound cars and trucks, but by exercising authority he controlled the flow of traffic. His authority was delegated to him by the local government and was represented by the badge and uniform he wore.

For the Christian, your badge has the name Jesus on it and your uniform is your identity in Christ. Instead of waving your arms and blowing your whistle, you use your words. Words have power when spoken in faith, within the will of God, and with the authority of who you are in Christ. They become commands or declarations and are powerful when aligned with God's Word and the promptings of the Holy

Spirit. Words have power.[2] God used words to speak the universe into existence. Proverbs tells us "Death and life *are* in the power of the tongue, and those who love it will eat its fruit" (Prov. 18:21).

The New Testament uses the metaphor of a sword, which of course is a weapon of war. Hebrews 4:12a states, "For the Word of God *is* living and powerful, and sharper than any two-edged sword …." The Amplified Classic Bible puts it this way: "For the Word of God is living and active *and* full of power [making it operative, energizing, and effective]." Later, in Revelation 1:16, the Bible gives additional information about this two-edged sword. Describing the ascended Jesus, the apostle John wrote: "He had in His right hand seven stars, out of His mouth went a sharp two-edged sword, and His countenance was like the sun shining in its strength."

Rick Renner, an eminent Greek scholar, unpacks this for us: "The phrase 'two-edged' is taken from the Greek word *distomos* and is unquestionably one of the oddest words in the entire New Testament. Why is it so odd? Because it is a compound of the word *di*, meaning two, and the word *stomos*, which is the Greek word for one's mouth. Thus, when these two words are compounded into one (*distomos*), they describe something that is two-mouthed!"[3]

A two-edged sword in the hands of a Roman soldier was a terrifying weapon. Paul's description of the sword as part of the armor of God (Eph. 6:17) describes it this way: "And take the helmet of salvation, and the sword of the Spirit, which is the Word of God …" Here the Greek word *rhema* is used for Word. A rhema word is "something that is spoken clearly, vividly, in unmistakable terms and undeniable language."[3] Putting this altogether, Renner concludes that when God speaks a word to you, the first edge on the sword is applied. God's spoken word, Scripture, is the first edge. This two-edged sword came out of Jesus' mouth, so we can conclude the second edge is put on the sword when we speak the word!

This is how and why your words spoken with authority are powerful weapons against the powers of darkness, including sickness and disease. If this sword is left in its sheath, it is of no value. It must be taken out and skillfully wielded to win victories and defeat the devil. This will only happen when God's word is hidden in your heart, and you wield it with authority.

I expect, for many this is new, and perhaps you are reluctant to step out and use your words of authority. Perhaps it will help knowing this is exactly what our Leader modeled for us. In Matthew chapter four we see Jesus being confronted by Satan Himself three times. How did He deal with His adversary? Each of the three times the Son of God said (out loud with His words), "It is written" followed by a specific Scripture that was a deadly two-edged sword against the attack (Matt. 4:4, 7, 10). I love what Jesus said in the third temptation: "Away with you, Satan! For it is written …" Please overcome any hesitancy you might have. This is the biblical war strategy for victory.

When you know you are sons and daughters, ambassadors with jurisdictional authority and responsibility, soldiers, and kings, you are equipped to use your authority when required. If you see yourself merely as a sinner saved by grace, a humble servant, there is an ungodly ineffectual bashfulness and timidity in fighting spiritual battles. This will never do if you want to be an effective minister of healing. Healing is part of the larger war between the kingdom of God and the kingdom of darkness.

It is important to have a historical perspective on this subject and see how it fits into the entire biblical narrative. It begins in the Garden of Eden. As I said in chapter four, God chose to use Adam and Eve in partnership to run things on the Earth. In Genesis 1:26-28, God stated that Adam was given dominion over the Earth. Psalm 115:16 adds to our understanding: "The heavens are the heavens of the Lord; the earth He has given to the sons of men." The Hebrew word translated *given* is *nathan,* which in this verse means "to give an assignment." It is saying that God will oversee the heavens, but the Earth He has assigned to mankind. The Passion Translation makes this abundantly clear: "The heavens belong to our God; they are His alone, but He has given us the earth and put us in charge."

You know what happened next: Adam sinned, and all of mankind followed suit. Adam's authority was surrendered (delivered) to Satan, who became "god of this age" and ruler of this world (Lu. 4:6). God's rescue plan was ingenious. Adam (a human) lost the authority, so a New Adam would have to regain it. This New Adam was sinless Jesus who would recapture authority over the Earth and therefore rule once again, both the heavens *and the Earth.* Jesus confirms this in Matthew 28:18-19: "All authority is now given to Me, both in heaven *and on earth...*" (emphasis mine). Three short scriptures summarize this redemptive plan beautifully:

> *"He who sins is of the devil, for the devil has sinned from the beginning. For this purpose the Son of God was manifested, that He might destroy the works of the devil" (1 Jn. 3:8).*

> *"Inasmuch then as the children have partaken of flesh and blood, He Himself likewise shared in the same, that through death He might destroy him who had the power of death, that is, the devil, and release those who through fear of death were all their lifetime subject to bondage (Heb. 2:14-15).*
>
> *"... having wiped out the handwriting of requirements that was against us, which was contrary to us. And He has taken it out of the way, having nailed it to the cross. Having disarmed principalities and powers, He made a public spectacle of them, triumphing over them in it" (Col. 2:14-15).*

Now that God had taken back the authority on Earth, He once again delegated it back to us, the church, the body of Christ.

> *"Behold, I give you the authority to trample on serpents and scorpions, and over all the power of the enemy, and nothing shall by any means hurt you" (Lu. 10:19).*
>
> *"And Jesus came and spoke to them, saying, 'All authority has been given to Me in heaven and on earth. Go therefore and make disciples of all the nations, baptizing them in the name of the Father and of the Son and of the Holy Spirit, teaching them to observe all things that I have commanded you; and lo, I am with you always, even to the end of the age.' Amen" (Matt. 28:18-20).*
>
> *But this Man, after He had offered one sacrifice for sins forever, sat down at the right hand of God, from that time waiting till His enemies are made His footstool. For by one offering He has perfected forever those who are being sanctified (Heb. 10:12-14).*

This phrase in Hebrews 10:13, "From that time waiting till His enemies are made His footstool" is very interesting. Jesus defeated Satan at the cross, but He is waiting for him to be put under His feet! This will be completed in its finality when Christ returns a second time to Earth. In the meantime, He is waiting for you and me to use our power and authority to rule on His behalf in our area of jurisdictional assignment.

Using the example of the policeman again, we know that any law enforcement entity has a specific jurisdiction in which they legally perform their duties. A city policeman has authority only within city limits. The county sheriff has authority only within his assigned county. The state police have no authority in another state. So, it is important you know your assigned area of responsibility—your jurisdictional realm of authority. All of us, as believers, have authority in our own lives, our marriages, families, places of work, and cities. This is clear. I learned in 2002 I had jurisdictional authority where the members of our church lived. This is authorized when you are prompted by the Holy Spirit and when you see works of evil that God wants you to deal with. He does this in partnership with you.

We know with certainty we have jurisdictional authority and power regarding sickness and disease. The Bible leaves no doubt. It is a work of the enemy, whether directly (see Matt. 8:16, 9:32-33, 10:1, 12:22, 15:21-28, 17:14-21; Lu. 4:39, Acts 19:12 etc.) or indirectly though the fall of humanity. We know because Jesus specifically gave it to us in Luke 10:19 and Luke 9:1-2. He was very specific in our assignment and jurisdiction: "Then He called His twelve disciples together and gave them power and authority over all demons, and to cure diseases. He sent them to preach the kingdom of God and to heal the sick."

These verses are the first edge of the sword. The second edge is sharpened when you begin to speak God's word with authority, which releases His power into the situation. I learned how to do this in our healing room in Mexico. Over and over, we saw results when we ministered healing in this way. There was a woman who had suffered from severe fibromyalgia for over ten years. Upon questioning, the Holy Spirit reminded her it began when she was ministering deliverance to another person in Mexico City ten years earlier. Suddenly, we had the key. I recited Scriptures so the enemy knew I knew he was defeated at the cross. I dealt with the matter by commanding with authority, "Devil, I release you from your assignment to this woman." It was that simple. She knew she was immediately healed as all symptoms left and have remained gone to this day. We had numerous other examples—healing of a torn meniscus, chronic back problems, a woman's chest injury received fifty years prior when a roof paving stone fell on her as a young girl, depression, painful breast lumps, and more. Some of the healings were instant and some were progressive. We believed, and told the person we prayed for, that something significant happened when we prayed. Oftentimes, this begins a process of healing that may take days, weeks, or months.

Power and Authority

Before moving on, let's combine the previous chapter (power) and this chapter (authority). As I've quoted many times, these are the two ingredients Jesus gave His disciples in Luke 9:1-2. Our illustration of a policeman brings these two critical elements together. In America, we call them Law Enforcement Officers. Let's look at each of these words separately and draw the spiritual application: Law ... Enforcement ... Officer.

The word *officer* tells us this man or woman is "a person holding a position of command or authority." This is represented visually by the uniform and the badge. Legally it is supported by their employment and authority delegated to them by their commanding officer.

Enforcement tells us this person has the power to enforce their authority in the line of duty. This is demonstrated visually by their gun, baton, handcuffs, taser, and radio. Their authority can be released in actual power if necessary. Authority without power is ineffective. Where power is not used, the bad guys will eventually take over!

Law tells us there are written rules and regulations the police officer is enforcing. It is not his or her haphazard ideas that are backed by their authority and power. What they are enforcing must be legal, passed by the rightful legislative body, and written down.

When officers are in their cars cruising around town, they are looking for any activity violating the law. When observed, they spring into action, using their authority and power to set things right, to bring order out of disorder, and to arrest any perpetrators who are violating the law.

This description should describe mature, trained Christians, having been deputized by Christ and who spring into action when they see the enemy violating the law of God. Sin, bondage, sickness, and disease should be seen as the kingdom of darkness encroaching on the kingdom of God. You have been deputized and equipped with all the necessary equipment:

Power: Baptized in the Holy Spirit with power (dunamis); the sword of the Spirit—Spirit empowered words, spoken and released with authority.

Authority: Using the name of Jesus and your identity as a son or daughter, ambassador, soldier, and king. "... that *at the name of Jesus* every knee should bow, of those in heaven, and of those on earth, and of those under the earth..." (Phil. 2:10, emphasis mine).

Radio—a direct line to the King of kings and promptings of the Holy Spirit. Jesus did what He saw the Father doing (Jn. 5:19).

So, it is time to put on your police uniform and enforce the laws of the kingdom—to become a Law Enforcement Officer for Jesus. Or, if you prefer ancient symbolism, it is time for some sword practice![4,5]

Additional Scriptures: Ex. 14:21, 17:8-13; Num. 20:7-8; Josh. 1:8-9; 1 Sam. 17:40-47; Matt. 8:16, 21:23-27; Mk. 11:12-14, 20-24; Lu. 4:1-13, 6:45, 8:1-3, Acts. 8:5-8, 9:40, 14:8-10; 2 Cor. 10:3-5; Heb. 2:5-8; 1 Jn. 4:4, 5:19; Rev. 5:2 (Amplified Classic Bible), 2:12, 12:11.

Questions to Consider:

1. Regarding the authority of the believer, how would you describe yourself … ignorant? somewhat familiar? or fully knowledgeable? Why? What was the most important thing you learned in this chapter?
2. Did this chapter expose any lies you believe?
3. Jesus displayed a beautiful blend of boldness and authority, humility and kindness. He knew when to use each. Do you? Think this through. Apply this to your family and areas of influence.
4. If you are "naturally" a quiet, merciful, kind person, has this become a stronghold in your life? Can you learn to be bold and use your authority when the situation calls for it?
5. How does your authority in the realm of healing affect the way you will pray for healing? See these New Testament examples: Jesus in Matthew 8:1-3, 26, 9:5-7, 21:19, John 11: 43-44; Peter in Acts 3:6-8, 9:32-35; Paul in Acts 14:8-10, to name just a few.
6. How can you begin to exercise your authority in your areas of jurisdiction?
7. Read Matthew 8:1-13 and see how Jesus used His power and authority to heal the leper and the Centurion's servant. What did Jesus say about authority and how can you apply what He said to the Centurion?

Chapter 8

The Kingdom of God

What was Jesus' central message during His three and a half years of ministry? If you asked John Doe on the corner of the street, he might say love or peace. If you asked your fellow church members, they would probably include the same two, but add such things as you must be born again, forgiveness, repentance, and prayer. I would be surprised if many would say *kingdom*. Herein lies the taproot of weakness and powerlessness in the church.

The full gospel is more than forgiveness for sins and eternal life. Jesus preached the *gospel of the kingdom*. He spoke about the kingdom of God over 120 times and mentioned the church (Gr. *ekklēsia*) but twice! This is shocking if you are like me, who heard little about the kingdom during much of my Christian life. Twenty-nine of Jesus' parables were recorded for us and twelve of them described the ways of the kingdom—the hidden treasure, pearl of great price, mustard seed, great banquet, ten virgins, talents, and workers in the vineyard, to name a few.

Many facets of the kingdom of God, or as Matthew called it, the kingdom of heaven, weigh heavily upon our subject of divine healing. They are, in fact, almost inseparable. Jesus performed thirty-seven miracles demonstrating the kingdom and twenty-seven of those were healings.

The concept of kingdom finds its roots in the prophetic words of Isaiah:

> *For unto us a Child is born,*
> *Unto us a Son is given;*
> *And the government will be upon His shoulder.*
> *And His name will be called*
> *Wonderful, Counselor, Mighty God,*
> *Everlasting Father, Prince of Peace.*
>
> *Of the increase of His government and peace*
> *There will be no end,*
> *Upon the throne of David and over His kingdom,*
> *To order it and establish it with judgment and justice*
> *From that time forward, even forever.*
> *The zeal of the Lord of hosts will perform this (Is. 9:6-7).*

Isaiah prophesied the birth of Christ and His government. When the bible speaks about a kingdom, it is speaking about a form of government.

Kingdom means the *king's domain*—his realm of ruling and reigning. It is the Greek word *basileia,* which comes from the word *basileús,* meaning king. Earthly kingdoms have defined geographical boundaries. The kingdom of God has no boundaries. It is the total and eternal reign of God over all creation. It is an invisible kingdom (Lu. 17:20-21) and an unshakeable kingdom (Heb. 12:28). It is the Father's good pleasure to give us the kingdom (Lu. 12:32). Jesus' purpose in coming was to preach the kingdom of God: "I must preach the kingdom of God to the other cities also, because for this purpose I have been sent" (Lu. 4:43).

The answer to my question above, *what was Jesus' central message,* is simply but profoundly this—*the kingdom of God.* Early in His ministry Jesus announced the kingdom of God had arrived: "Now after John was put in prison, Jesus came to Galilee, preaching the gospel of the kingdom of God, and saying, 'The time is fulfilled, and the kingdom of God is at hand. Repent, and believe in the gospel'" (Mark 1:15). This informs us that the doorway into the kingdom is repentance—turning from self-government and submitting to God's government; turning from the ways of this world to the ways of Jesus.

As citizens of His kingdom:

This is our **prayer**: "Your kingdom come. Your will be done on earth as it is in heaven" (Matt. 6:10).

This is our **priority**: "But seek first the kingdom of God and His righteousness, and all these things shall be added to you" (Matt. 6:33).

This is our **purpose**: "And this gospel of the kingdom will be preached in all the world as a witness to all the nations, and then the end will come" (Matt. 24:14).

This is the **model we follow**: "And Jesus went about all Galilee, teaching in their synagogues, preaching the gospel of the kingdom, and healing all kinds of sickness and all kinds of disease among the people" (Matt. 4:23).

This last point leads into the relationship between divine healing and the kingdom of God. It is set forth in the scriptural theme of this book, Luke 9:1-2. If you were to thoroughly study and analyze the kingdom of God, volumes would be written. For this chapter, however, Matthew 4:23 and Luke

9:1-2 act as magnifying glasses, concentrating the meaning into this short but important idea—the kingdom of God is a kingdom of power and authority manifesting itself in healing the sick and setting captives free. Jesus had one central message, and it was validated by the works He performed.

My principal aim in this chapter is to transition you, my reader, from a church mindset to a kingdom mindset. This does not mean to diminish the importance of the church by any means. *"Basileia* or kingdom is God's end —the goal of Christianity. *Ekklesia* or Church is God's means—the method of Christianity. Thus, the kingdom descends in order that the Church may ascend."[1] It is not the kingdom or the church, but both/and.

A church mindset usually thinks in terms of ministries (small groups, bible studies, youth, children), Sunday sermons, worship, discipleship, serving, fellowship, and outreach. These are important in growing as Christians, becoming family, making disciples, and sharing the gospel.

A kingdom mindset brings an entirely new dimension to your calling and purpose as a believer. It develops a cosmic perspective which brings into focus the purposes of God and the ministry of Jesus. You begin to see the battle between Satan and God, between the kingdom of darkness and the kingdom of light. It brings new and powerful tools to bear on living a victorious Christian life.[2] A kingdom mindset is about the government of God outside the four walls of the church as well as inside. God wants to rule in your life, your family, your place of work, the nation, and all parts of society. When your mind is renewed to kingdom thinking the power of God can be released into the realms of life and culture.

To grasp the implications and power of identity, it is important to expand your perspective from church to kingdom. Personally, I have only begun to do this in the last few years, enhancing my understanding of Scripture, my walk with God, and my ministry of healing.

The identities of son, ambassador, soldier, and king have been highlighted because they enable and empower Jesus' commission to heal the sick and deliver those in bondage. A revelation of the kingdom is inseparable from the ministry of divine healing.

These four identities speak of action. Understanding the Hebraic view of kingdom will bring a full understanding to this. Jesus, being a Jew, would have been thinking in a Hebraic way as He taught and demonstrated the kingdom. David Bivin and Roy B. Blizzard, in their excellent book *Understanding the Difficult Words of Jesus,* reveal the Hebrew concept of kingdom:

> *The concept of "Kingdom" is perhaps the most important spiritual concept in the New Testament. In English or Greek, "kingdom" is never verbal. It is something static, something to do with territory. But in Hebrew, "kingdom" is active, it is action. It is God ruling in the lives of men. Those who are ruled by God are the Kingdom of God.*
>
> *Kingdom is also the demonstration of God's rule through miracles, signs, and wonders. Wherever the power of God is demonstrated, there is His 'Kingdom.' How can one see God's Kingdom? It is only possible when 'kingdom' is correctly understood as something which is verbal not static. <u>We see God's Kingdom when we see Him in action</u>. This is what Jesus meant when He said: "...if it is by the finger of God that I cast out*

> *demons, then the Kingdom of God has come upon you" (Luke 11:20)."*[3]

With this understanding, let's see how these four identities come alive with meaning and purpose:

Sonship: As a son or daughter, you assume responsibility in administering Father's business. You are not an observer but a participant. Jesus did (action) what He saw His Father doing (Jn. 5:19-20). Jesus' ministry was a ministry of doing—using His power and authority to heal the sick and set the captives free. As part of the family business, we now walk in His shoes proclaiming the kingdom and advancing it through teaching with signs following (Mk. 16:20, Heb. 2:3-4). This has little relevance in a church-centric worldview.

Ambassador: This identity has new meaning as you represent (re-present) the kingdom of God to the kingdom of darkness and a world governed by the god of this age. You have ambassadorial power and responsibility given to you by your King as soon as you walk out your front door. Wherever you go you are on assignment, the chosen representative of your home country in a foreign land. Within your family you have the responsibility of making your home an embassy of heaven. Even more than this, you have been specifically sent with guidance from the king (president or prime minister) to be his representative in all matters of governmental importance. Again, this has little relevance in a church-centric mindset.

Soldier: When you were born again, you were born into a war between two kingdoms. Soldiers are trained in the art of war to fight battles and win victories. In my experience, few Christians have taken on the identity and responsibility of being soldiers as spiritual warfare is understood and practiced only in small pockets of the body of Christ. This has prevented many from winning their battles and living victorious lives. An understanding of kingdom makes the soldier identity an essential aspect of life. As the kingdom advances, battles must be fought and won on all fronts—your life, marriage, family, church, work, city, and nation. You are fighting from a position of victory but fight you must. Paul's description of the armor of God in Ephesians six suddenly takes on greater significance. This is most clearly seen and acted upon with a kingdom mindset, not a church mindset.

King: Kings rule and reign in their territorial jurisdiction. They have both power and authority. My example in chapter seven where the rapist was caught soon after our kingly authority was exercised is a powerful picture of taking responsibility when evil encroaches on your territory. As a believer, you are seated in heavenly places in Christ (Eph. 2:4-6), equipped and commissioned to exercise your authority and power in the jurisdictions assigned to you. This concept has little relevance in a church-centric worldview.

Hebrews 10:12-13, in context of the kingdom, paints a fuller picture of the importance of teamwork with the Godhead—Father, Son, and Holy Spirit: "But this Man, [Christ] after He had offered one sacrifice for sins forever, sat down at the right hand of God, from that time *waiting till His enemies are made His footstool*" (emphasis mine). Jesus is waiting for us, the church[3], to do our part—a new concept for many of us! This exposes another lie that is often believed about our relationship with God and what He expects of us.

Many have been brought up in a church environment of do's and don'ts with an emphasis on how to live. Christianity is living in relationship with Father's love through Christ. In many circles the "work of ministry" in Ephesians 4:12 has little to do with proactively extending the kingdom of God as Jesus did in His ministry. This has led to patterns of passivity where Christianity is largely composed of going to church, listening to a sermon, and serving in a ministry or two on a Sunday morning. My friend, Jesus is waiting for you to make His enemies His footstool!

The kingdom of God brings together the previous chapters of this book into a cohesive system of belief and action. The glue holding everything together. This is the spiritual reality activating and releasing a full understanding of what it means to be a Christian—not just in character, but in action and ministry. This action is not to earn God's favor but arises from the place of rest in His love.

The kingdom has a direct bearing on healing when viewed through the lens of governmental matters—two kingdoms vying for supremacy. When a disease shows up in a body, it is a coup d'état, an illegal and overt attempt to unseat the rightful governmental authority. It is the kingdom of darkness attempting to overrule God's kingdom rule in the person. Jesus came to destroy the works of the devil. The ministry of healing is the ministry of using the power of the Holy Spirit and your authority to overrule this governmental entity and once again establish the kingdom of God's rule in this person. (see Matt. 12:28-29, Mk. 3:23-27, Lu. 11:20-22). When you exercise your governmental authority as ambassadors and defeat sickness, you are putting Jesus' enemies under His feet. Hallelujah!

This chapter serves only as the briefest introduction to the kingdom of God as it relates to the ministry of healing. I've provided Scriptures below for further study. Additionally, I recommend Jack Taylor's book, *Cosmic Initiative: Restoring the Kingdom, Igniting the Awakening*[4] for an in-depth study of the kingdom. Bill Johnson's book, *When Heaven Invades Earth*[5] weaves the kingdom throughout his powerful book.

At the outset of this book, in my acknowledgements, I mentioned that my wife and I participated in a seven-day cruise hosted by Jack Taylor. For the final twenty years of his life, Jack was consumed with understanding the width and depth and power of the kingdom. Participating in this cruise and being immersed in his knowledge and understanding was a profound experience for us. Jack passed away at eighty-seven, shortly after finishing his seminal work, *The Cosmic Initiative*.

I want to close this chapter with a selection of our notes from the cruise.

- You were made for the kingdom. Refuse to settle for any other. Don't allow any other kingdom or pursuit to win your loyalty, fill your passion, or distract your search for the greatest things in life. No other kingdom will answer life's pressing problems or solve the mystery of the reason for your existence on Earth. No other kingdom is eternally relevant. If you seek anything besides God's kingdom, you are trafficking in nothingness, flirting with idolatry, and consorting with futility. Conversely, when you seek God's eternal kingdom, you seek all that matters.
- Repent, the kingdom of God is at hand. Receive it. If you don't, you will be stuck in every wrong idea or thing you think you're right on. You must decide between what you think you know and absolute truth.

- Your God is too small.
- The kingdom is God's family business and is a Father-son paradigm. Make sons, not orphans.
- The enemy has no fear of a kingdomless church.
- Repentance is the measure of your revelation. The greatest gift is the grace of repentance. Kingdom life is a repenting life.
- God, what do I need to straighten out? Change my mind on everything where I do not see eye-to-eye with you.
- Entrance into the kingdom is by faith. The dynamic of the kingdom requires excavation.
- When you study the kingdom, storms start coming. The enemy fears power. The kingdom is forever under assault.
- Remember that the war to which the kingdom beckons you has already been won.
- What we seek first will determine what our lives will be like.
- Seeking the kingdom of God and His righteousness before everything else is the key that unlocks all benefits available in heaven and on Earth.
- The phrase "defeated Christian" is really an oxymoron. We lose only when we stop fighting.
- Only kingdom thinking and kingdom living can overcome the effects of the fall of humanity.
- Jesus suffered His way to wholeness, lost His way to winning, and died His way to life, thus bringing back to this Earth the expression of the eternal enterprise of the kingdom of God.

- The gospel of salvation is a truncated gospel. The church has lost its kingdom mentality and thus its kingdom theology and practice.
- Our part is to prepare our minds to receive kingdom mentality, our hearts to embrace kingdom living, and our lives to receive kingdom power in the Holy Spirit to transform our culture.

May these short quotes motivate you, as they did us, in pursuing the kingdom of God in a deeper way. It is a great adventure.

Additional Scriptures: Dan. 2:43-44; Matt. 3:1-2, 13:10-11, 13:19-30, 19:13-14, 24:14; Mk. 1:14; Lu. 8:1, 9:62, 22:26-30; Jn. 3:3, 18:36; Acts 1:1-3, 8:12, 14:21-22; Rom. 14:17; Gal. 5:19-21; Col. 1:13-14, 4:11; 1 Thess. 2:10-12; 2 Pet. 1:10-11.

Questions to Consider:

1. How has this chapter affected your thinking about the Christian life?
2. Has this brief teaching about the gospel of the kingdom affected your understanding of the gospel? What will change?
3. What areas of your responsibility (jurisdiction) will be affected by what you have learned? How?
4. Romans 5:17 says you are to "reign in life" through Jesus Christ. Looking back over your life, are there areas of defeat that might have been different with a personal revelation of the kingdom? If so, let this change your future.

5. Do you understand the need for spiritual warfare more clearly—why you cannot ignore it and why it is important to face your battles and win your victories?
6. In light of the kingdom, have your personal identities become more important in living an effective and fruitful life for Christ?

Chapter 9

Summary in One Word

We have come to the final chapter. This has been building to a crescendo that can be expressed in one word. Before I get to that, it is important to summarize briefly the main points in the book. I remember in bible college how I was taught that a good preacher first tells his audience what he will be preaching, then he preaches it, and finally he summarizes what was taught.

Chapter one described why the ministry of healing is important. Healing the sick was at the center of Jesus' ministry because Jesus' message was the kingdom of God. If you want to become a disciple of Christ and a participant in His ministry, you cannot avoid the ministry of healing the sick and delivering those taken captive by the devil. There are at least five critical reasons this ministry must be embraced—healing right now!

1. The Great Commission: the gospel that will be preached before the end comes is the gospel of the kingdom. Christ wants His bride to be complete,

composed of those from every nation and every tongue. This is a season of bringing in the harvest which necessarily includes a powerful move of the Holy Spirit with healing, signs, and wonders. A display of God's power will create kerfuffles, opening opportunities for the gospel, and opening the eyes of the spiritually blind.

2. The glory of God: When the power of God is manifested, His glory is on display for all to see. The sick are healed and those in bondage set free, not by church programs or plans of men, but by the power of God. He is glorified.
3. Christ's compassion: God is love. Jesus was God in the flesh. His compassionate heart fueled His ministry of setting men and women, boys and girls, free from sin and sickness.
4. The 4th and 5th reasons are the Church's faith: We are living in troubled times sucking faith from multitudes of hearts. Paul wrote our faith should not be in the wisdom of men but in the power of God. This is important as the baton is passed from one generation to the next. Our children and grandchildren must see and experience firsthand the power of God in their lives to be strong in faith in the presence of an onslaught of secular humanism.

Chapter two looked at seven reasons to believe it is always God's will to heal. Doubts in this area have left Christians' faith weakened with unbelief. It is unlikely any ministry of healing will be effective if the prayer minister's heart is contaminated with unbelief.

God's name (Jehovah Rapha) and nature define Him. We can rest assured that He is the same today as He was in Exodus when He revealed His name to the children of Israel.

1. Atonement, as revealed in Isaiah 53:4-5, clearly states our sins are atoned for by the blood of Christ, and provision for our healing was made through His broken body. Jesus confirmed this interpretation, in Matthew 8:16-17, and Peter again confirmed it in 1 Peter 2:24. As biblical scholars, Jesus' and Peter's interpretation of Isaiah's prophecy should remove all doubt.
2. Sickness came in on the back of Satan's work of deception with Adam and Eve when sin was introduced into the bloodstream of the human race. The root issue of all humanity is sin, and the being behind sin is Satan. In Jesus' ministry we see sin and sickness closely connected, seeing Him regularly dealing with both at the same time. At the cross Jesus destroyed the works of the devil. When the root off sin was dealt with sin, so was the fruit of sickness.
3. Jesus, our elder brother, healed every person who came to Him seeking healing and deliverance. He turned none away. This reason alone should settle the issue for His followers, who desire to please Him and walk in His footsteps. The baton was then passed to His disciples. Our goal should be to do what our Rabbi taught and demonstrated for us.
4. The Lord's prayer, as it perfectly describes His will. "Your kingdom come. Your will be done on earth as it is in heaven." When the kingdom of God has fully come as His rules in any situation, then Earth will re-

flect heaven. No sickness or bondages in heaven. No sickness or bondages on Earth. This is the goal.

5. The confirmation of the apostle James. If you are sick, call in the elders and have them anoint you will oil, and the prayer of faith will save the sick. This begins in James 5 verse 14 by saying "Is any among you sick?" If there is *anyone* sick? Anyone is anyone! There are no qualifications here.
6. Your personal identity as a sheep—a sheep belonging to the flock of the Great Shepherd. The heart of every good shepherd is to love and care for his sheep. No earthly shepherds compare with the love, compassion, and power of Jesus.

The following six chapters highlight common areas where massive numbers of Christians believe things "that make the word of God of no effect" (Mk. 7:8, 13). Believers must have their minds renewed according to Scripture, not their personal experiences nor the traditions of their church denomination.

Chapter three revealed the true nature of God. Many Christians see God's fingerprints on sickness, disease, and bondage. No, He is not involved in making (or allowing) a person to be sick. It is against His word, His character, and His will. God's sovereignty should not become the rug under which we sweep unanswered questions, unanswered prayers, or unresolved disappointments. His true nature is seen in the man and ministry of Jesus Christ. Full stop.

New Testament Scripture reveals how God disciplines His Children this side of the cross—not with sickness, disease, accidents, or tragedies, but with His word, spoken by the Holy Spirit directly or through others.

Chapter four set forth the importance of personal identity. There is a war on identity across all spectrums of society. A Christian must move beyond being a mere sinner saved by grace and a humble servant into identities that embrace power and authority—sons and daughters, ambassadors, soldiers, and kings. These facets of a complete in-Christ identity equip and enable believers to effectively minister healing.

Chapter five highlighted that when Jesus uttered His last words on the cross "It is finished," it was finished! The work of redemption was completed. The sinless Lamb dying substitutionally in our place released all the benefits that flow from the lavish gospel of grace. When ministering healing to others, we need not ask God to do something He has already done. The gospel of grace released a flood of unearned benefits to mankind which are received by faith alone. This includes divine healing.

Chapter six brought into focus the necessity for Holy Spirit power and partnership. When Jesus launched His disciples into their ministry of healing in Luke 9:1-2, He gave them power and authority over demons and to heal the sick. This power is received with the baptism of the Holy Spirit, first given to the church in Acts chapter two. We release the Holy Spirit power that's in us when we minister healing. God can and will do more than we can ask, think, or imagine, but He does it "according to the power that works in us" (Eph. 3:20).

Chapter seven described the believer's authority. Without exercising your Christ-given authority, little will be accomplished in bringing God's will from heaven to Earth. At the cross Jesus destroyed the works of the devil (1 Jn. 3:8). However, the enemy continues to operate until the follower of

Christ uses his or her authority to enforce the defeat. Authority is likened to a double-edged sword wielded when you speak God's word and His will into situations, bringing those out of order into biblical order. Too many Christians have become accustomed to a passive role of asking God to do something He has assigned them to do.

Chapter eight introduced Jesus' central message of His ministry—the gospel of the kingdom. Kingdom mindsets and lifestyles are critical for the release of power and authority through understanding of personal identity. As you migrate your focus from a church-centric mindset, you will become more effective in your God-given ministry of kingdom matters, of which healing is preeminent.

Faith

With these eight chapters under your belt, you now have a solid foundation and a robust belief system upon which you can build and grow. I'm sure you can guess the one-word summary these chapters all point toward—FAITH. Faith is the currency of the kingdom; the currency by which you buy and sell (receive and release) goods in the kingdom of God. Faith is the action by which you make withdrawals from your heavenly bank account. God deposited into your account every spiritual blessing by grace. We withdraw them by faith.

Hebrews 11:1: "Now faith is the assurance (title deed, confirmation) of things hoped for (divinely guaranteed), and the evidence of things not seen [the conviction of their reality—faith comprehends as fact what cannot be experienced by the physical senses]" (AMP). Faith comprehends as fact what cannot be seen, felt, or heard. The basis of this reality is found only in the word of God. This is why your mind must be renewed by the word of God—not the traditions of men or your personal experiences.

In all the training my wife and I have received over the years, the road we have traveled has been the road from hope to faith. "The great majority of Christians who seek healing seek it only in hope, but not also in faith, so they do not receive it. In other words, they may want to receive, but they haven't made their requests relying on the basis and qualifications for healing that are provided in God's word. I have to be brutally frank about this. They are seeking healing on the basis of hope, but they have omitted the prerequisite of faith. They may not even know the difference between the two. What God has promised of faith, He has not made available to hope apart from faith."[1]

Hope is a very necessary part of a healthy Christian life, one of the big three: "And now abide faith, hope, love, these three; but the greatest of these is love" (1 Cor. 13:13). Hope is a confident expectation of a coming good. Hope is future oriented and is in the mind. Faith is the assurance, the reality, here and now in your heart of things that you are hoping for in the future—promises in the word of God given to you as His child, such as healing (Rom. 10:17). Hope is not weak faith but is important in its own right.

In Jesus' ministry of healing, we see faith inextricably linked to healing. Here is a small selection:

- "Assuredly, I say to you, I have not found such great faith, not even in Israel" (Matt. 8:10)!
- "When Jesus saw their faith, He said to the paralytic, 'Son, be of good cheer; your sins are forgiven you'" (Matt. 9:2).

- "But Jesus turned around, and when He saw her He said, 'Be of good cheer, daughter; your faith has made you well.' And the woman was made well from that hour" (Matt. 9:22).
- "Then He touched their eyes, saying, 'According to your faith let it be to you'" (Matt. 9:29).
- "Then Jesus answered and said to her, 'O woman, great *is* your faith! Let it be to you as you desire.' And her daughter was healed from that very hour" (Matt. 15:28).
- "So Jesus answered and said to them, 'Assuredly, I say to you, if you have faith and do not doubt, you will not only do what was done to the fig tree, but also if you say to this mountain, 'Be removed and be cast into the sea,' it will be done'" (Matt. 21:21).

These Scriptures demonstrate healing is released through faith. Faith must be on the scene, actively operating in the one praying, the one receiving, or a third party. If *you* have faith, you can pray for the lost or those with little or no faith. You, as the one ministering, can release your faith to the one in need. Look at Acts 3:6-7, where faith-filled Peter released healing to the man born lame (no faith). And when Jesus yelled, "Lazarus, come forth" his body obeyed even though dead men have no faith!

Faith operates through a third person in the example of the centurion who came to Jesus on behalf of his servant (Matt. 8:5-13). It is again seen when the Gentile mother came on behalf of her daughter (Matt.15:21-28) and the ruler who came to Jesus when his daughter had died (Matt. 9:18-26).

This is exciting stuff! It opens the door for healing to take place through your faith on the streets and in the marketplace.

One time I prayed for our Muslim Uber driver while visiting our family in England. When we got into the car, I observed that Mohammed had a back brace and was clearly in pain. When we arrived at the train station, I removed our bags from the car and asked him about his back. He said he had chronic back pain since childhood. I told him I was a Christian and asked if I could pray for his back. He said yes, as they almost always do. With his permission, I gently laid my hand on his lower back, released my faith by thanking God for what He was about to do, and commanded the back to be healed and the pain to go. After this 60-second prayer, I asked him to begin to move his back and see how it felt. He was stunned—out of pain for the first time in years! It wasn't his faith of course, but mine. This is the power of the kingdom, touching the lost and bringing glory to Jesus. I can only imagine the conversation when he arrived home.

To conclude our brief discussion of faith, let's examine what may be the greatest adventure of faith in Scripture—the patriarch of our faith, Abraham. God called him, at seventy-five, out of his country, while making a covenant with him to make him a great nation, to bless him, and to make his name great (Gen. 12:1-3). This of course meant that he and Sarah would have a son at a ripe old age. This promise was a great test of their faith. *Really? How is that even possible at our age?* And then time passed … and passed … and passed. Then we come to Genesis eighteen. At ninety-nine years of age, God appeared to Abram once again, confirming His covenant, renaming him Abraham. Sarah laughed at the possibility. Can you imagine waiting twenty-five years for this promise? His was faith that endured (Heb. 6:11-15).

This brings us to Romans 4:18-22 where Paul describes the story.

> *"... [Abraham] who, contrary to hope, in hope believed, so that he became the father of many nations, according to what was spoken, 'So shall your descendants be.' And not being weak in faith, he did not consider his own body, already dead (since he was about a hundred years old), and the deadness of Sarah's womb. He did not waver at the promise of God through unbelief, but was strengthened in faith, giving glory to God, and being fully convinced that what He had promised He was also able to perform. And therefore "it was accounted to him for righteousness."*

We learn several important things here. Abraham and Sarah must have awakened each morning, looked in the mirror, and thought, *God, are you kidding?* But they persisted, "... contrary to hope, in hope believed ... And not being weak in faith, he did not consider his own body, already dead." To walk in faith and win your victory, you must look beyond your circumstances. You don't deny them, but they fade into the background when eyes of faith see the promise.

"Abraham did not waver at the promise of God through unbelief, but was strengthened in faith, giving glory to God." Abraham was steadfast, immovable, and his faith was strengthened as he gave glory to God before he saw the promise fulfilled. Your faith can grow, progress, and become strong as you keep our eyes on the One who promised.

"And being fully convinced that what He had promised He was also able to perform." Here we see the definition of faith in full bloom. Abraham became *fully convinced* of the promise. Why? Because God was able to perform! He promised it. He would fulfill His promise.

What an example to inspire you in your personal walk of faith. The writer of Hebrews picks up on Abraham's situation when he says, "And we desire that each one of you show the same diligence [as Abraham] to the full assurance of hope until the end, that you do not become sluggish, but imitate those who through faith and patience inherit the promises. And so, after he had patiently endured, he obtained the promise" (Heb. 6:11-12, 15).

My goal in writing is to equip an army of believers in an effective ministry of healing the sick. However, if you need healing, everything written can be applied personally. Healing is your inheritance. Receive it by faith. It is as much your right as forgiveness of your sins.

Healing Right Now is intended to be your on-ramp, or a quick start guide, to launch your ministry of healing. Once you begin, you will want to grow and expand your understanding into other areas not covered in this book. I suggest three books for you to consider as your next steps. First, is Barry Bennett's book, *He Healed Them All.*[2] This book will cover this subject of divine healing from A to Z in more depth than I chose to do here. It is excellent. Then there is Derek Prince's book, *God's Word Heals*.[3] Derek was a pioneer in healing and deliverance in the 20th century. His writing is simple but deep. This is a wonderful book. Lastly, I would recommend Dr. Henry Wright's book *Exposing the Spiritual Roots of Disease.*[4] Dr. Wright was a trailblazer in connecting the dots between spirit, soul, and body in disease, disease prevention, and healing.

Launching out in this ministry is an adventure. You will experience great joy and times of disappointment. Your knowledge and skills will improve. Some will be healed immediately and some gradually. I like what Derek Prince says about this: "You may be instantaneously healed, or you may receive a healing that begins. If it begins, keep your plug into God's power outlet. If you say, 'I didn't get healed; nothing happened,' do you know what you have done? You have pulled the plug out. If you say, 'God touched me, and I'm going to keep thanking Him until its complete' it will be complete."[3]

Undoubtedly, not everyone you pray for will be healed. So, how do you handle this for you and the person being ministered to? First, keep on keeping on. Don't allow discouragement to set in. There must always be a place given to ... *there are things I don't fully know or understand (in general or specific to the situation), a mystery only God fully knows.* Seek Him for more understanding and wisdom. If you lose a battle, it doesn't mean the war is over! Keep fighting.

In this book, I have endeavored to reduce this mystery from something expansive to something quite small. As we all grow in a greater revelation of the six topics identified in chapter two, and additional ones you will discover for yourself, your skills and understanding will improve, and your success rate will grow. We all must become more mature and skillful in understanding and applying the word of God (Heb. 5:13). As we do, our faith will grow, and our ministry will be more effective. The Scriptures speak of no faith, weak faith, faith, and great faith. Remember, Jesus told the centurion, "Assuredly, I say to you, I have not found such great faith, not even in Israel! Go your way; and as you have believed, so let it be done for you" (Matt. 8:10, 13). We are all on an adventure toward great faith!

There is also the subject of God's fresh anointing and His power being present for healing (Luke 5:17). Yes, healing is a finished work, but the Holy Spirit is also proactively involved. As His presence and power are increasingly manifested in this hour, we will see greater and greater manifestations of His glory.

It is also helpful to remember love is the greatest and most important matter. If things don't turn out the way you expect, Paul's exhortation to us is important: "For now we see in a mirror, dimly, but then face to face. Now I know in part, but then I shall know just as I also am known. And now abide faith, hope, love, these three; but the greatest of these *is* love" (1 Cor. 13:12-13). Love leaves no room for condemnation or judgmentalism. Continue to praise Him, asking from more insight and revelation.

Paul's words in Acts 20:24 have become my personal mission statement. I'd like to close with this: "But none of these things move me; nor do I count my life dear to myself, *so that I may finish my race with joy*, and the ministry which I received from the Lord Jesus, to testify to the gospel of the grace of God" (emphasis mine).

Don't give up. The only defeat is if you quit! You have the word of God on your side and the Holy Spirit in you. You have the finished work of Christ as your foundation and the Great Commission propelling you. The love of God is being poured out all over the Earth, and it is a privilege to partner with Him in this season. Use your authority and power to extend the kingdom of God and make the enemies of Jesus His footstool.

Additional Scriptures: Hab. 2:4; Matt. 6:10, 8:26, 9:2, 9:22, 9:28-29, 14:31, 15:28, 17:17, 17:20, 21:21, 25:21; Mk. 5:36, 9:23-24, 11:23-24, 16:17; Lu. 16:10-11, 17:5-6, 18:8; Acts 3:16, 6:5, 6:8, 11:23-24, 14:9, 16:5, Rom. 1:8, 1:17, 3:22, 10:17, 11:20, 12:3, 12:6; 1 Cor. 2:5; 2 Cor. 5:7; Gal. 2:20, 3:14, 5:6; Eph. 2:8, 3:17, 6:16; 2 Thess. 1:11; 1 Tim. 6:12, Heb. 4:2, 11:1-40; Js. 1:6, 2:18; 1 Pet. 1:5; 2 Pet. 1:1; 1 Jn. 5:4.

Questions to Consider:

1. What encouraged you most in this chapter?
2. Considering the six aspects of a consistent belief system discussed in chapter two and reviewed in this chapter, what were the most important truths you learned? Why?
3. Now that you have finished the book, what lies were exposed that made the word of God of no effect in your life and ministry? Be specific. Rejoice that they were uncovered.
4. Do you feel you are prepared to set out on the adventure of healing the sick? How do you think Jesus' disciples felt when He sent them out for the first time?
5. Has your faith been strengthened while reading this book? Are you excited to begin this adventure?
6. What questions still remain that you want answered? See if Appendices A and B answer these.

Appendix A

How to Minister Healing

We often talk about "praying for the sick." I propose a better way to describe this is to "minister healing to the sick." When we think of praying for something, in most people's minds, it means petitioning God *for* something or *to do* something. Considering everything presented in this book, this is not the most biblical way to minister healing.

There are two examples in Scripture where we might see praying for the sick. First is Lazarus' resurrection from the dead. Jesus' loud and bold command to the dead body of His friend "Lazarus, come forth!" produced a miracle. Not many of us would consider Jesus' command a prayer! But in the two verses prior to Jesus' declaration, we read this: "Then they took away the stone from the place where the dead man was lying. And Jesus lifted His eyes and said, "Father, I thank You that You have heard Me. And I know that You always hear Me, but because of the people who are standing by I said this, that they may believe that You sent Me."

Jesus was in constant communion and communication with His Father. In this instance, He spoke these words out loud so those observing would know the Father sent Him. So, in a sense, He was praying, but what raised His friend from the dead was a bold command, not a prayer of petition.

Second, is the well-known passage in James chapter five—calling for the elders of the church to come and pray for the sick. Specifically, it says "... and let them pray over him, anointing him with oil in the name of the Lord. And the prayer of faith will save the sick and the Lord will raise him up" (Js. 5:14-15). This is a beautiful passage full of information. There are many types of prayer the elders might consider praying—prayers of thanksgiving (for what He is about to do, for the presence of the Spirit, and the power to heal), prayers of adoration ("hallowed by your name"), and prayers of authority and declaration. All of these are wonderful and appropriate. I would be certain, however, that these first century elders would not have been praying "if it by your will."

Over the past few years, my wife and I have prayed for and ministered healing to hundreds and hundreds of men and women, boys and girls. There is no formula. I don't want to suggest there is. However, throughout this book, I have described the biblical aspects of this ministry. We have Jesus' example (twenty-six different documented occurrences of healings) and those of the apostles. From this comes an overwhelming consensus of general principles that are biblical and effective. This is confirmed by the success of modern-day men and women who have followed in the footsteps of Jesus and the apostles.

Before a word is said to the one you are ministering to there are three important matters. First and foremost is to have the eyes of your heart on Jesus, who is the author and perfector of your faith (Heb. 12:2). As Jesus had His eyes on His Father, our eyes are on Jesus. He is the source of the flow of all goodness and power for healing. Yes, healing is a completed work, but we must remember that Christ is the vine, and we are the branches. We remain in Him, abiding in Him so the sap of the flow of life will flow through us.

The second follows from the first—be listening to the Holy Spirit. Cultivate your listening ear. Each person and situation is unique. Expect Him to speak. The Lord loves this person more than you do and knows everything not seen. He knows the keys to their full restoration. This is why having a prayer partner is important also. My wife, who accompanies me most of the time, is sensitive to the Spirit. Two are better than one in this ministry of healing.

Third, step into every situation with confidence, knowing who you are in-Christ and what you have been given. You have the same Spirit, the same Scriptures, and the same power and authority Jesus gave His apostles. Know God is with you, and the Holy Spirit is leading you. Be confident if you do your part, you can leave the results to the Lord. Know you are the devil's worst enemy! Have the attitude and expectancy as you minister, you are releasing the power and authority in you to the one in need of healing. You are following Peter's model in Acts 3:6. Confidence, or assurance, is very important and can be found in the definition of faith in Hebrews 11:1: "Now faith is the substance of things hoped for, the evidence [or confidence] of things not seen." Most other translations use the English word *assurance*.

Have confidence knowing sickness, just as sin, is Jesus' enemy, and you have been called to put His enemies under

His feet. Have confidence healing is a governmental matter and you represent the greater, more powerful government, the kingdom of God.

It is often good to begin with a question:

- "What is it you want us to pray for?"
- "What are you believing for that we can agree with?"
- "When did this begin?"
- "What was going on in your life when this started?"

Answers to inspired questions often hold the key to anointed ministry.

Oftentimes we share one or two Scriptures or an encouragement to build the person's faith—Scriptures such as Proverbs 4:20-22, Psalm 103:1-3, Isaiah 53:4-5, Matthew 8:16-17, or God's name, Jehovah Rapha. Perhaps we'll share a brief personal testimony. Be prepared! Memorize these and other verses because you won't always have your bible on hand. By memorizing these Scriptures, and others, you will also be meditating on them and strengthening your own faith.

Thank the Lord for this person, and for carrying this condition or illness on Himself on the cross. "Lord, we pray into this situation now … we speak life, healing, and wholeness. I release *healing right now* into this matter." Remember, you are releasing what Jesus already provided and deposited in you. Sometimes it is not even your words but the laying on of your hands, if given permission and appropriately placed, and thanking the Lord for healing this person two thousand years ago.

Use your authority, and speak directly to the situation, the injury, body part, or illness, and tell it what it must do! Jesus spoke to the fig tree and said, "If you speak to this mountain …" (Mt. 21:20-22). When Jesus healed Peter's mother-in-law of her fever, He rebuked the fever using His authority. If appropriate, you can say, "God, I take authority over this matter and command this sickness to go;" or "I command this back to come into alignment ..." You can use your authority to command something to go that should not be in the body, such as fever, infection, cancer etc. or to move or repair parts of the body into proper position, like backs, joints, and injuries.

After our prayer and ministry, it is biblical and recommended to ask the person to do something they could not do before—move their back, bend their knee, breathe deeply, or walk. In the process of action, you will frequently see improvement or complete healing. We ask the person if they feel any different. Any change? This is a biblical pattern (Acts 3:7-8, Acts 9:41, Mark 1:31). Thank the Lord for any improvement.

Just as we launched the healing room in Mexico, we prayed for a lady at church who had a torn meniscus. She was in pain and on crutches. Our ministry to her was as I described above. After a short time of ministry, she was walking up and down the stairs to the stage, and within a day or two was totally healed. No surgery necessary. This gave us confidence and momentum as we began the healing room in our small Mexican village.

In Luke 13:10-17 Jesus loosed a woman who was afflicted with a spirit of infirmity for eighteen years. Yes, an evil spirit of infirmity can afflict a person. In our experience this is often revealed if the person has many afflictions going on at the same time. If we sense this, I will simply and directly deal with it as Jesus did, with the authority I have been given over all the power of the evil one. "Spirit of infirmity, I command you to go, in the name of Jesus;" or "I release you now from your assignment to this person." These are not merely words, but words of authority and power released by faith—spiritual power against a spiritual enemy.

There can also be hindrances to healing and spiritual roots of diseases. God is interested in our sanctification, as well as our physical healing. He often wants to get to the root of the matter not just the fruit. These roots may be sin issues, personal wounds of the soul, or trauma. The first one to consider is unforgiveness. This is the most prevalent. If you feel prompted, bring this possibility up. Unforgiveness and bitterness can be a root of arthritis and a hinderance to healings of all sorts.

Experienced ministers of healing have discovered that the person's complaint may itself be a metaphor or a picture of what the root cause is. One example we learned is hip joint problems. Many people who want prayer are facing hip replacement. This is very common. As strange as it may sound, oftentimes this person was required, early in life, to take on responsibility beyond their years—to carry their family "on their hip" so to speak. If this is confirmed, ask the person if they are ready to forgive their parent(s), followed by praying for healing of their soul and releasing any wounds they may have experienced. After this has been cleared away, minister healing to their hip. Rely on the Holy Spirit to prompt you in matters like this.

I bring this up as one example of the connection between the soul and body. If the ministry opportunity affords the time, we have found success in asking the Holy Spirit to bring to the person's mind any "high octane," in a negative sense, issues from their past. Frequently, there were harmful relationships, traumatic events, or deep sin issues. The Lord wants to heal their soul-wounds as well, and one often leads to the other. Once again, a valuable resource to pursue this further is Dr. Henry Wright's book, *Exposing the Spiritual Roots of Disease.*

This leads to a final subject I will briefly mention—generational iniquity and family curses. Many years ago, I began to understand this by learning from Derek Prince. His book, *Blessing or Curse, You Can Choose* is a great place to start. Generational iniquity is a real thing. It is apparent we inherit physical traits from our parents, grandparents, and on up the line. Generational influences have the potential to bring blessings or curses on one's life.

In Exodus 20:5-6, God warns the children of Israel not to follow false gods: "... you shall not bow down to them [false gods] nor serve them. For I, the Lord your God, am a jealous God, visiting the iniquity of the fathers upon the children to the third and fourth generations of those who hate Me, but showing mercy to thousands, to those who love Me and keep My commandments."

If one's ancestors have been into evil and sinful things, consequences can fall on the following generations. This is particularly potent when there has been involvement in the occult, freemasonry, alcoholism, and pornography. The following illustration is helpful in envisioning what may be going on: two teenage boys are exposed to pornography. One shakes it off knowing it is not something he should get involved with and gets on with his life with no major problems. The second boy is hooked and finds himself locked into a very strong bondage. What is the difference? The second boy has an invisible, metaphoric backpack he is wearing which contains the inherited weight of this sin package from the generations above him.

I have a personal example of inherited generational weakness. For years, while I was a pastor, I had an over-the-top fear of confrontation. In certain situations, I became paralyzed with fear. I knew it was irrational but was powerless to rid myself of it. Along the way I discovered that my grandfather, whom I greatly admired, had the same bondage. While my wife and I were taking Henry Wright's course, *For My Life*[1] we were working through the subject of fear with respect to generational iniquity. Holy Spirit brought my grandfather to mind. Bingo! After a short time of praying into this, repenting, and breaking this generational iniquity with the blood of Jesus, I was set free! Totally free. That quick. Something I had struggled with for years was gone.

The first question that may come to your mind is this: *but I thought Jesus became a curse for us?* Let's look at this more closely, in Galatians 3:10-14. This passage is about the curse that comes when a believer rejects grace and willingly falls back under the law. As no one can keep all the law, they open themselves to a curse. Then in verses 13-14 Paul wrote: "Christ has redeemed us from the curse of the law, having become a curse for us (for it is written, 'Cursed *is* everyone who hangs on a tree'), that the blessing of Abraham might come upon the Gentiles in Christ Jesus, that we might receive the promise of the Spirit through faith." In context, this means New Testament believers are not under the law but under grace. Being under grace, we have a better covenant that comes from Abraham by faith, and we receive the blessings, including the Holy Spirit, flowing from God's covenant with him.

A curse does not have *legal right* to afflict us any longer as sons and daughters, purchased and redeemed by the blood of Christ. This becomes your weapon to break any curse or family iniquity that has come down the family line. This is parallel to understanding 1 John 3:8 I described in chapter four. John wrote that Jesus Christ came to destroy the works of the devil. This does not mean he is not actively attacking Christians but means he has no *legal right* to do so. You, therefore, must enforce Christ's victory over him. The same is true of curses and inherited iniquity. You must enforce the power of the blood of Christ, removing and destroying that invisible backpack. How? By using the power of repentance and the authority you have been given, all of which this book has equipped you to do.

To wrap up this discussion on how to minister healing to the sick, I want to return to James chapter 5, which I mentioned earlier in this appendix. Let's go deeper by looking at two Greek words. James 5:16 in the New King James (NKJV) and the New Living Translation (NLT) say this:

> *Confess your trespasses to one another, and pray for one another, that you may be healed. The effective, fervent prayer of a righteous man avails much. (NKJV)*
>
> *Confess your sins to each other and pray for each other so that you may be healed. The earnest prayer of a righteous person has great power and produces wonderful results. (NLT)*

The Greek word translated *effective, fervent* in NKJV and *earnest* in the NLT is *ischuo*. "It is embodied strength that 'gets into the fray' (action), i.e. engaging the resistance. For the believer, it refers to the Lord strengthening them with combative, confrontive force to achieve all He gives faith for."[2] The word translated *avails much* (NKJV) and *produces wonderful results* (NLT) is the Greek word *energeo*. It means "To energize, working in a situation which brings it from one stage to the next, like an electrical current energizing a wire, bringing it to a shining light bulb."[2] Put together, James 5:16b, in expanded Greek reads this way: "Very combative (engaging, overcoming) is the specific (urgent) request of a divinely-approved person who is energized (by God)."[2]

This summarizes the energy and power involved when you minister healing to the sick. You may not feel anything, but you are dangerous, wreaking havoc on the kingdom of darkness. As a faith-filled child of God, knowing who you are in Christ, and having been biblically trained, you are sickness' and the devil's worst enemy!

Appendix B

What About Paul's Thorn in the Flesh?

One of the most effective strategies of the devil is to plant seeds of doubt in the hearts of God's children. This began in the garden of Eden when he whispered to Eve, *hath God said*? His attacks are primarily focused in three areas—the character and identity of God (Father, Son, and Holy Spirit), believer's in-Christ identity, and the word of God. He is always warring against faith, causing doubt and unbelief. He wars against the plain and simple truth found in Scripture. In recent years the theory of evolution has been used to plant doubts in the hearts of countless Christians. A thorough study of creation science debunks evolutionary theory and extinguish the devil's arrows of fire. So, it is no surprise that he would attack your faith concerning healing in any way whatsoever.

One of the verses I have highlighted in this book is from Jesus' debates with the religious leaders of Israel. They twisted the true meaning of Scripture and "made the word of God of no effect" (Mk. 7:13). In many church circles, Paul's thorn in the flesh is often held up as evidence God uses sickness and disease to discipline or humble His people. His fingerprints are seen on situations needing healing and deliverance. If this is a misunderstanding of Scripture, as I believe it is, then it is one of today's primary examples of making the word of God of no effect. Here are the relevant verses from 2 Corinthians 12 that we must consider:

> *"Of such a one I will boast; yet of myself I will not boast, except in my infirmities" (verse 5).*
>
> *"And lest I should be exalted above measure by the abundance of the revelations, a thorn in the flesh was given to me, a messenger of Satan to buffet me, lest I be exalted above measure. Concerning this thing I pleaded with the Lord three times that it might depart from me. And He said to me, "My grace is sufficient for you, for My strength is made perfect in weakness." Therefore most gladly I will rather boast in my infirmities, that the power of Christ may rest upon me. Therefore I take pleasure in infirmities, in reproaches, in needs, in persecutions, in distresses, for Christ's sake. For when I am weak, then I am strong (verses 7-10).*

Paul had received many powerful revelations and was taken into the third heaven where he heard words he could not express (2 Cor. 12:2-4). On the surface, it appears Paul was made sick to keep him humble. "Many will say, 'If Paul's sickness was from God maybe mine is as well.' Instantly, the revelation of the cross, of redemption, of Jesus' ministry, the healing gifts given to the church, the miracles in the book of

Acts, and the revelation of God's nature throughout the Bible are discarded, and Paul's thorn is exalted as 'Exhibit A' in the case against divine healing."[1]

Let's see if there is an alternate explanation harmonizing it with the full weight of Scripture as presented in the previous nine chapters. Personally, I am not willing to tear up everything else the bible says regarding healing to accommodate the vague situation Paul was describing.

First, whatever Paul was describing as "a messenger of Satan," was not a messenger from God. To understand what Paul described as a thorn in the flesh, we should first allow Scripture to interpret Scripture. Similar language is used elsewhere in the Old Testament, in which Paul was a scholar. The word *thorn* appears fifty-two times in the bible. Forty-eight times it is used literally. Four times it is used metaphorically—Numbers 33:55, Joshua 23:13, Judges 2:3, and Ezekiel 28:24. The first three metaphorical usages all refer to the same situation, the enemies that remained in the land of Canaan that Israel did not drive out. They were left in the land and became "thorns" in their side. We understand what this means. The verse in Ezekiel is very similar. There the Lord was speaking through the prophet saying He would destroy one of Israel's nearby enemies, Sidon. When He did, they would no longer be a painful thorn for Israel. It is clear from these four instances of a thorn in the side of Israel, it was used metaphorically and had nothing to do with sickness.

I believe Paul was using his thorn in the flesh metaphorically in a similar way, consistent with Scripture. Paul was describing constant "reproaches, needs, persecutions, and distresses" (verse 10 above). Paul's opposition, the ones persecuting him, were thorns in his flesh. (See for example

Acts 13:50, 14:1-5, 19-20, 16:19-22, 17:1-15, 18:12-13). This would also explain his use of the word "infirmities" in verses 9 and 10, which is the NKJV translation for "weakness" and the same word used earlier in the verse 9. This Greek word can mean weaknesses due to sickness, but it also can mean suffering and calamity. The trials and tribulations Paul suffered were relentless and exceedingly difficult to bear. He listed them in the previous chapter (again, the contextual application is important):

> *Are they ministers of Christ?—I speak as a fool—I am more: in labors more abundant, in stripes above measure, in prisons more frequently, in deaths often. From the Jews five times I received forty stripes minus one. Three times I was beaten with rods; once I was stoned; three times I was shipwrecked; a night and a day I have been in the deep; in journeys often, in perils of waters, in perils of robbers, in perils of my own countrymen, in perils of the Gentiles, in perils in the city, in perils in the wilderness, in perils in the sea, in perils among false brethren; in weariness and toil, in sleeplessness often, in hunger and thirst, in fastings often, in cold and nakedness—besides the other things, what comes upon me daily: my deep concern for all the churches. Who is weak, and I am not weak? Who is made to stumble, and I do not burn with indignation? If I must boast, I will boast in the things which concern my infirmity [weakness] (2 Cor. 11:23-30).*

In the context of his second letter to the Corinthians and the Old Testament usage of thorns, Paul is, in all likelihood, talking about the unbearable trials and persecutions he had to endure. He asked the Lord to take them away from him. The Lord responded, "My grace is sufficient for you," because

Christ carried sin and sickness on the cross, not persecution and trials.

The final matter to discuss is different than the one above. Paul describes what appears to be a physical ailment in his letter to the Galatians:

> *You know that because of physical infirmity I preached the gospel to you at the first. And my trial which was in my flesh you did not despise or reject, but you received me as an angel of God, even as Christ Jesus. What then was the blessing you enjoyed? For I bear you witness that, if possible, you would have plucked out your own eyes and given them to me (Gal. 4:13-15).*

There is a reasonable explanation for this that Barry Bennett brings out in his book[2]: "Paul's ministry to the Galatian region occurred during his first missionary journey, which is described in Acts 13 and 14. In this account of Paul's ministry and journey, we can find no evidence of Paul being sick. However, there is one event that does give us a clue as to Paul's sufferings.

> *Then Jews from Antioch and Iconium came there; and having persuaded the multitudes, they stoned Paul and dragged him out of the city, supposing him to be dead. However, when the disciples gathered around him, he rose up and went into the city. And the next day he departed with Barnabas to Derbe (Acts 14:19-20).*

This took place in the region of Galatia. Paul was stoned and left for dead, but God raised him up! From there he departed to Derbe, a town in Galatia. Could it be the letter to the Galatians is referring to this event and Paul's subsequent recovery from being stoned? I believe so. Perhaps the rocks struck his head and face caused swelling around his eyes. Since we have no mention of Paul being sick during this journey, I would suggest the stoning was the affliction which he had to fully recover."

Finding examples of someone sick or recovering from injury in the New Testament does not in any way detract from the ministry of divine healing. God designed our bodies with natural immunity and the ability to heal themselves. This often takes time or an adjustment in lifestyle. Injuries can also take time to heal naturally, and this is probably what was happening to Paul. Not many of us have had to recover from stoning!

As one final defense of my position on this, Philippians chapter three sheds additional light. From verses 7 to 11 Paul gives us a powerful description of everything he gave up to follow Jesus. This was a fulfillment of the prophetic word Jesus gave him through Ananias in his dramatic salvation on the road to Damascus. Jesus said "Go, for he [Paul] is a chosen vessel of Mine to bear My name before Gentiles, kings, and the children of Israel. For I will show him how many things he must suffer for My name's sake" (Acts 9:15-16). Now back to Philippians 3:10: "… that I may know Him and the power of His resurrection, and the fellowship of His sufferings, being conformed to His death …" Paul shared in the sufferings Jesus experienced. He listed those exhaustively in 2 Corinthians eleven and twelve and other places. Jesus NEVER suffered from sickness and disease prior to the cross when he bore them for the whole world. And neither did Paul.

Our first port of call for interpreting Scripture is Scripture itself. The traditional interpretation of Paul's thorn in the flesh, which contradicts the seven reasons to believe it is always God's will to heal I proposed in chapter two, should be examined carefully. Is there an alternative interpretation of Paul's situation? One should be suspect of an interpretation that, in one go, sweeps aside the weight of Scripture and makes the word of God ineffective. The above explanation sheds light on this and provides a consistent biblical theology of divine healing.

End Notes

Introduction:

1. Mayer, Gary, *Stolen Identity: Christian Who Are You?* Copyright ©2022 (Published by Gary Mayer).

Chapter 2: Reasons to Believe God Still Heals Today

1. McCrossan, Dr. T.J., *Bodily Healing and The Atonement;* Re-Edited by Dr. Roy Hicks and Dr. Kenneth E. Hagin; Copyright © 1982 (Rhema Bible Church).

Chapter 3: The True Nature of God

1. Marcus, *Warren M., The Priestly Prayer of the Blessing;* Copyright ©2018 (Charisma Media/Charisma House Book Group, 600 Rinehart Road, Lake Mary, FL 32746), Kindle edition.
2. Johnson, Bill; *God is Good: He's Better Than You Think;* Copyright ©*2016* (Destiny Image Publishers, Inc.; P.O. Box 310, Shippensburg, PA. 17257).
3. Wommack, Andrew; *The True Nature of God*; Copyright ©1997, 2010 (Andrew Wommack Ministries, Inc., P.O. Box 3333, Colorado Spring, CO 80934).

Chapter 4: Identity

1. Quote taken from The Gospel Coalition (TGC) blog *Tozer vs. Lewis: What's The Most Important Thing About Us?* by Justin Taylor, June 4, 2016.
2. Mayer, Gary, *Stolen Identity.*

3. Johnson, Bill; *When Heaven Invades Earth: A Practical Guide to a Life of Miracles;* Copyright ©2003; (Treasure House, an imprint of Destin Image Publishers, Inc., P.O. Box 310 Shippensburg, PA 17257).
4. Mayer, *Stolen Identity*, chapter one.
5. Jordan, James; *Sonship: A Journey Into Father's Heart*; Copyright ©2014 (Fatherheart Ministries, www.fatherheart.net).
6. Hill, Stephen; *Our True Identity: An Interpretation of Galatians;* Copyright ©2024, (Fatherheart Ministries 2024).

Chapter 5: Healing is a Finished Work

1. William Barclay's commentary on John is excellent. He describes John chapter 1 this way: "The first chapter of the Fourth Gospel is one of the greatest adventures of religious thought ever achieved by the mind of man." He gives great insight into Jesus being called the l*ogos* of God. His commentary "Daily Study Bible" can be found online at www.bibleportal.com.
2. I recommend Joseph Prince's book, *The Healing Power of The Holy Communion,* Copyright ©2020, (Emanate Books, an imprint of Thomas Nelson; Nashville, TN).

Chapter 6: Holy Spirit Power and Partnership

1. Wright, Dr. Henry W., *Exposing the Spiritual Roots of Disease* ©2019 by Be In Health® (Whitaker House 1030 Hunt Valley Circle, New Kensington, PA 15068).
2. Prince, Derek, *God's Word Heals;* © 2010 by Derek Prince Ministries International; pg. 141.

Chapter 7: Believer's Authority

1. Sheets, Dutch, GiveHim15.com, February 15 post.
2. Derek Prince has a powerful template of a healing proclamation. I reproduce it here for your consideration:

> *"My body is a temple of the Holy Spirit; redeemed, cleansed, and sanctified by the blood of Jesus. My members, the parts of my body, are instruments of righteousness yielded to God for His service and for His glory. The devil has no place in me, no power over me, no unsettled claims against me. All has been settled by the blood of Jesus. I overcome Satan by the blood of the Lamb and the word of my testimony, and I love not my life unto the death. My body is for the Lord, and the Lord is for my body."*

3. Renner, Rick, *Sparkling Gems from the Greek*; Copyright ©2003 by Rick Renner; P.O. Box 702040; Tulsa, OK 74170; p. 109, Feb. 22 reading.
4. I highly recommend Derek Prince's book *God's Word Heals*.
5. Barry Bennet's book *He Healed Them All* is excellent and he writes about our authority in Christ in an enlightening way. Published by Harrison House, Shippensburg, PA.

Chapter 8: The Kingdom of God

1. From notes taken on Alaska cruise with Jack Taylor on the subject of the kingdom; September 2014.
2. David Bivin, Roy B. Blizzard, *Understanding the Difficult Words of Jesus,* ©1983 Makor Foundation, (Arcadia, CA 91006); p. 90-91.

3. The Greek word for church is *ekklesia.* In early Greek culture the *ekklesia* was a called-out group who governed, made laws, and dictated foreign policy. After Jesus said, "I will build my church" in Matthew 16:18, in verse 19, He said: "And I will give you the keys of the kingdom of heaven, and whatever you bind on earth will be bound in heaven, and whatever you loose on earth will be loosed in heaven." These tools are part of our arsenal in advancing the kingdom and winning victories. For further study I highly recommend Dutch Sheets' widely read book Intercessory Prayer, published by Bethany House, a division of Baker Publishing Group.
4. Taylor, Jack, *Cosmic Initiative: Restoring the Kingdom, Igniting the Awakening*; ©2017 Dimensions Ministries, Melbourne, FL (Whitaker House, 1030 Hunt Valley Circle, New Kensington, PA 15068).
5. Johnson, *When Heaven Invades Earth.*

Chapter 9: Summary in One Word

1. Prince, Derek, *God's Word Heals*; p. 30.
2. See Rom. 5:17, 8:37, 1 Cor. 15:57, Eph. 3:20-21, Phil. 4:13, Jn. 10:10, 1 Jn. 5:4.
3. Bennet, Barry, *He Healed Them All.*
4. Prince, *Derek, God's Word Heals.*
5. Wright, *Exposing the Spiritual Roots of Disease.*

Appendix A: How to Minister Healing

1. *For Your Life* is an on-line program (or personal retreat) offered by Be In Health, Thomastan Georgia; www.beinhealth.com.
2. *HELPS Word-studies*; Copyright © 2021 Discovery Bible; Accessed by biblehub.com.
3. Prince, God's Word Heals; p. 169.

Appendix B: Paul's Thorn in the Flesh

1. Bennett, *He Healed Them All,* p. 215-216.
2. Bennett, *He Healed Them All*, p. 222.

GARY MAYER

Pastor Gary has 34 years of ministry experience since God called him out of the business world in 1990. This calling started an adventure that began with planting and leading a church in the UK for 20 years. This was followed by 10 years on the mission field in Baja California (Mexico) where he taught church planters, preached, began a healing room ministry along with his wife Barb, and started his writing career, in response to the Lord saying, "begin to write." His first book, *Imitate Paul*, was written primarily for church planters. The second, *Paul's Gospel*, was written to give believers a revelation of grace. The third, *Stolen Identity*, teaches on the critical importance of one's identity in Christ. Together they form a trilogy for discipleship and maturity in the local church.

Healing Right Now is written to meet an important and urgent need to equip an army of regular believers in the ministry of healing and catching a wave of the Holy Spirit beginning to move across the nations.

Made in the USA
Middletown, DE
22 May 2024

54366127R00086